W9-BQY-407

Lauriat's
BOOKS
BOSTON • CHESTNUT HILL
NORTHSHORE • SOUTHSHORE
BURLINGTON

Time in Greek Tragedy

Time in Greek Tragedy

Jacqueline de Romilly

PROFESSOR OF GREEK LITERATURE
AT THE SORBONNE

Cornell University Press

ITHACA, NEW YORK

First published 1968

Library of Congress Catalog Card Number: 68–16380

PRINTED IN THE UNITED STATES OF AMERICA
BY KINGSPORT PRESS, INC.

Acknowledgments

This book consists of six lectures which I delivered in April 1967 at Cornell University as Messenger Lecturer. This occasion, the purpose of which is indicated at the end of the volume, was for me both a great honor and a great pleasure; and I should like first of all to say how grateful I am to the University for favoring me with this invitation and to Professor Gordon M. Kirkwood and the members of the Department of Classics, whose constant kindness I shall never forget.

They have also helped me in getting the manuscript ready for publication. I am particularly indebted to Professor Kirkwood, who read the manuscript through and corrected many mistakes in language or presentation.

I should also like to thank the staff of Cornell University Press for the care and understanding with which all the practical problems were dealt with and the text clarified. Thanks to their advice, it has been possible to prepare a text which can be read without any knowledge of Greek, the original texts and references being all kept for the footnotes, as well as the more scholarly discussions.

Finally I should like to mention that the editors of the "Cornell Studies in Classical Philology" have allocated funds to defray part of the printing costs; thus it has been possible to give more complete footnotes, which may help scholars and students. I am deeply grateful for that generosity.

JACQUELINE DE ROMILLY

Ithaca, New York
April 27, 1967

Contents

Introduction 1

1 The importance of time in Greek tragedy 3

✣ *Time and tragedy* 5

✣ ✣ *Tragic crisis in Aeschylus, Sophocles, Euripides* 12

✣ ✣ ✣ *The refusal of time* 24

2 The personification of time in Greek tragedy 33

✣ *The absence of a mythological tradition* 34

✣ ✣ *Time in its relation to us* 41

✣ ✣ ✣ *Time in its relation to events* 49

3 Time in Aeschylus 59

✣ *The lessons of time* 60

Divine punishment, 60; wisdom, 67

✣ ✣ *The structure of the plays* 71

Trilogies, 71; the different plays, 72; Agamemnon, 77; the relation with Thucydides, 82

4 Time in Sophocles 87

✣ *The action of time* 88

Unsteadiness, 88; man's fortune, 89; man's feelings, 97

✣ ✣ *The answer of man* 102
Humanism, 102; heroic refusal, 103; confirmation by time, 106

5 Time in Euripides 113

✣ *Ancient doctrines* 113
Aeschylus' doctrine weakened, 113; Sophocles' trust weakened, 116; Sophocles' pessimism increased, 118

✣ ✣ *Time and emotion* 122
Impatience, 122; relief, 125; sorrow, 127

✣ ✣ ✣ *Remedies and compensations* 131
Oblivion, 131; memory, 135

6 Young and old in Greek tragedy 143

✣ *Aeschylus* 144
The old, 144; the young, 148; conflict, 149

✣ ✣ *Sophocles* 150
The sorrow of old age, 150; conflict, 154

✣ ✣ ✣ *Euripides* 158
The pathetic quality of age, 158; pure, heroic youngsters, 166; the problem of contemporary Athens, 168

Index 175

Time in Greek Tragedy

Introduction

Although interest in Greek literature has continued through centuries, each age looks for something different in it and reads it with a different understanding. Nowadays a characteristic tendency is to study this literature in its historical development, and to find in it evidence showing how the Greeks progressively discovered and made more precise many of the intellectual, moral, and political notions which still live on—for they were to give birth to our modern civilization.

Such an evolution is reflected in the whole of Greek literature, from Homer to Christian authors. But one could say that the fifth century B.C. was the time when these notions underwent the strongest transformation and where it is easiest for us to follow their development. And tragedy is, of all the literature of that century, the place where this transformation shows in the most striking manner. First, tragedy deals with everything that really matters in life, and conveys about life more than one meaning. But also, Greek tragedians have given us a number of plays, which follow one another with fairly well-known dates, and cover just about the whole century, from Athens' victory over the Persians down to her own final downfall. There the growth of ideas can be read almost year by year and can be brought into relation with the general evolution of the city.

One of the reasons why, among these ideas, time has been chosen as a subject for the present research is obvious. Time is now, for us, a central notion. We see it everywhere. We live in an age that is aware of history. And we generally tend to think about everything in terms of evolution and development. We have become conscious of this importance of time. Our literary authors (as Proust), our philosophers (as Bergson), have started to explore the meaning of time. Anthropology and psychology also deal with it. I was therefore tempted to see how the matter stood with the Greeks. And it seemed that whatever could be learned from them in that respect might, in any case, acquire more interest by reason of this general curiosity.

But I do not mean that tragedy is used here as evidence only—far from it. For the study of a theme which is central and the demonstration of a progressive development from one author to another would be expected to provide, ultimately, a new angle from which to look at ancient tragedies and perhaps a new manner of illustrating their inner structure and meaning. Were it but to invite a number of persons to read them anew and enjoy the reading, the aim would be sufficient and the research would be worth making.

1 The importance of time in Greek tragedy

Much attention has been given recently to the study of time in ancient Greece, particularly after the publication of Hermann Fraenkel's work on the idea of time in archaic literature, first published in 1931.[1] Among the most important and precise studies in that field are those of E. Degani and S. Accame, both of which appeared in 1961.[2] All of them point to one main idea, which is that originally the Greeks did not have a very clear idea of time. They did not speak of it much—in Homer the word

[1] Hermann Fraenkel, "Die Zeitauffassung in der archaischen griechischen Literatur," *Beilagenheft zur Zeitschrift für Ästhetik und allgemeine Kunstwissenschaft, XXV* (1931), 97–118, republished in *Wege und Formen frühgriechischen Denkens* (Munich, 1955), pp. 1–22.

[2] E. Degani, 'ΑΙΩΝ *da Omero ad Aristotele* (Padova, 1961); S. Accame, "La concezione del tempo nell'eta omerica e arcaica," *Rivista di Filologia e d'Istruzione Classica*, N.S. XXXIX (1961), 359–394. One should add B. Onians, *The Origins of European Thought about the Body, the Mind, the Soul, Time and Fate* (2d ed.; Cambridge, Eng., 1954), 411 ff.; and M. Treu, *Von Homer zur Lyrik, Wandlungen der griech. Weltbildes im Spiegel der Sprache* (Munich, 1953).

is never the subject of a verb; in Hesiod it does not appear; and, if we leave aside orphic poetry, which requires some discussion, it is mentioned only occasionally in ancient philosophers.[3] Practically, the idea of time does not appear to have been an important one before the fifth century, where at last it has pride of place, both in Pindar and in Greek tragedy. Greek tragedy is, in a way, at the end of an evolution: Hermann Fraenkel stopped there.[4]

Our theme should therefore be an interesting one, in two different ways.

First, if the consciousness of time was acute and ripe then, it means that each of the three great authors of tragedies must have views about it, both spoken and unspoken, which will show in their works. Indeed they do mention *chronos:* the word itself recurs more than four hundred times in the extant tragedies. We shall be able to see exactly what each of them thought about time, and to compare his thought with that of the others, thereby grasping something important in their personal philosophy.

But at the same time it is unlikely that the development of the idea of time should really end with tragedy. Even if tragedy is not wholly different, in this matter, from modern times, and does not strike us, at first sight, as implying a different psychology, one may assume that it retains some marks of its former development and some

[3] We have just one mention in Thales (A 1, Diogenes Laertius, I, 35; see below, p. 36) and one in Heraclitus (fr. 52: see below, p. 36). As regards time in Greek philosophers, one should add other names to the titles given above, particularly, among recent studies, J. de la Harpe, "Le progrès de l'idée de temps dans la philosophie grecque," in *Festschrift zum 60 Geburtstag von A. Speiser* (Zurich, 1945), pp. 128–137.

[4] E. Degani goes down to the hellenistic period, and yet he gives but one short chapter (12 pages) to "tragedy, comedy and prosa"!

features showing that the evolution has not yet been brought to an end. In that respect, tragedy, although it has never received much attention from the scholars who have studied the general evolution of the idea of time, should provide us with a new approach and illustrate with a new example the way in which the Greeks were continually making notions clearer and more precise, thus paving the way to our modern conceptions. That is to say, we shall hope to get a better understanding not only of the authors and their works, but of the history of ideas and of the growth of modern psychology.

This, indeed, is a promising aim. But I am not going to try to reach it immediately. For the particular position that tragedy seems to have in the evolution of the idea of time deserves, before all, some attention. And, if tragedy was born precisely when the consciousness of time became ripe and the idea of time important, it is worth inquiring whether this was just chance and whether the very structure of tragedy has not something to do with this state of things. In other words, it may be worth trying to see whether Greek tragedy as a whole does not exhibit some features that are in harmony both with this new importance of time and with the idea of an unfinished development.

❖

Time shows through change; and in that respect it is obvious that tragedy deals with time. Its subject matter is always one great event, which overthrows all that existed before: it means death, destruction, reversal of fortune; its strength rests on a contrast between before and after; and the deeper the contrast, the more tragic the event. This is why so many people, in tragedy, comment about time and its action; and this is why we find so many remarks on the fact that this subversive action could be foreseen or could not. Pindar speaks about time because he wishes to escape from its dangers; people in tragedy speak about it because they have not been able to escape from these dangers. There is no tragedy that does not deal with time.

Yet, this is no special privilege of tragedy. Many other forms of literature deal with similar events—in first place, the epic. What, then, is the difference?

The difference is well known; it was known already to Aristotle, when he said, first, that tragedy considered but a limited portion of time, and next that it was to reproduce a noble and complete action. Both these ideas have to do with time.

The first one is practical. Aristotle says in the *Poetics* that, whereas the epic has no limit in time, tragedy must, as far as possible, keep to one single revolution of the sun. Now this limit is certainly not true of all tragedies, as J. C. Kamerbeek recently has shown as regards Aeschylus.[5] But it is none the less true on the whole, and important. For it means that tragedy centers on one action and follows this action continuously from beginning to end.

The epic tells many tales. It settles in an undeterminate past and goes backwards and forwards freely, putting all things on a level. It offers, in turn, scenes at home and scenes of battle, goes from Troy to the tent of Achilles or

[5] "Aspecten van de Tijd in de Grieske Tragedie, Speciaal big Aeschylus," *Medelingen der Kon. Nederl. Akademie*, N.S. XXVI (1963), 147–158.

Agamemnon, stops for a narration or a parenthesis. On the contrary, tragedy settles in a clear portion of time and obliges us to live along with it, minute by minute, as if it were the present. Being a direct imitation of life, with no storyteller between us and the action, it has to follow the experiences and emotions of the characters in their very continuity. Therefore it goes, without stopping, from beginning to end, according to the inner rhythm of time.

And the result is that the action becomes, as Aristotle says, serious and complete (*spoudaia kai teleia*): all has been made to bear on one and the same issue, which thus acquires importance, and makes sense; for we see how it progresses, what are its dangers, and what its results. This sequence creates a sort of tension: tragedy always represents a crisis.

I think the difference can be made clear by two examples.

I was very much struck by Gordon Kirkwood's comparison of the passage in Sophocles where Ajax bids farewell to his son with the parallel scene in Homer. Kirkwood finds in the wife's speech in Sophocles an "immeasurably greater tension, rhetorical emphasis, compression and urgency." [6] This contrast, I think, agrees perfectly well with the difference in literary form. In Homer, we have, among other scenes, the description of a queen, worrying because her husband goes to fight among other heroes. In Sophocles, the interest is focused on a captive woman, whose companion is on the verge of committing suicide. The danger is greater. But also, since the beginning of the play, we have heard nothing but this

[6] "Homer and Sophocles' Ajax," in *Classical Drama and Its Influence* (London, 1965), p. 58.

woman's anguish. We know how much is involved in the answer she wants to get. Hence the increased tension. In fact, urgency must appear as soon as the epic is turned into tragedy.

And if this urgency shows in the scene I have just mentioned, it ought to be kept in mind that the example was a very special one: for, there, the epic was so tense and concentrated as to be appropriate for transposition into tragedy. This is very seldom the case. And in the extant tragedies there is no other example of so close an imitation —perhaps, precisely, because the difference of structure and of literary form made too wide a difference.

Let us think, for instance, of the famous quarrel between Agamemnon and Achilles, which opens the *Iliad:* where could we find something equivalent in tragedy? Naturally we have some quarrels in tragedy: Agamemnon and Menelaus quarrel about Iphigeneia's life, Menelaus and Peleus about Andromache's; but these quarrels do not arise freely, or develop freely: they are connected with what we knew; they are made to bear on an issue which the whole tragedy follows and which involves life or death for one of the characters.[7] Indeed, they are but a sharper and tenser discussion of the impending action and crisis.

Practically, tragedy offers but one example of a quarrel which seems to go on for its own sake and become important in itself: that is Medea's quarrel with Jason. But even there, the quarrel takes a particular feature from the very development of action in tragedy.

[7] The quarrel in the *Iliad* is of even greater consequence; but we do not know this when we read of the quarrel and we shall be allowed to forget it quite often.

When Medea first sees Jason, we have already known her for 445 lines. We have been made aware of her rancor and despair: we have first heard about them, then heard her complaints, then seen Medea herself and heard all about her feelings. Then we have seen the King, Creon, arriving with a new threat which suddenly gives a character of urgency to Medea's anguish. Now she decides to have her revenge; and she must have it quickly, for she has obtained just one day of delay before leaving the city: "One day! allow me to stay but one day," she says in line 340. And this is a strict limit: something terrible must happen during the following hours. "I tell you: if the next light of the sun-god sees you still within the bounds of this country, you will die," declares the King; "During this day, I shall make corpses of three of my enemies: the father, and the girl, and also my husband," declares Medea. And it is in that atmosphere, on these premises, that Jason finally appears—after we have been associated in a steadily increasing anxiety about his fate and hers, and about their reciprocal hatred. This continuous and regular progression, where one single problem gets more and more urgent till it bursts into crime, is the very core of tragedy.[8] We see the difference from the epic. For the quarrel now not only explains a decision of major importance (it does, in both cases): it also has acquired a new dimension by the sheer fact that we have been prepared for it by what came

[8] This, of course, does not show with equal clearness in all tragedies. A tragedy like the *Trojan Women*, for instance, is made of several different actions, as if it were part of an epic poem. This possibility will be dealt with later (pp. 23–24). But, even in such cases, it will be noted that these actions are all made to bear on one single emotion—Hecuba's—which is followed in its continuity: all the episodes gather around her and join with each other as parts of her sorrow.

before; it has become part of a whole development where before and after are included, and which leads without any respite from one to the other: ultimately, the progression ends in violent death and the action is, as said Aristotle, *teleia*, that is to say, complete, or final.

Such a structure is therefore something quite different from the epic. And it was, in Greek literature, something new. Now it seems only logical that it should have arisen precisely when the consciousness of time was getting clearer and stronger. Tragedy summons our emotion by following a crisis in its continuous and unavoidable growth.

But this is not all. In fact, we shall have to explain both the word "crisis," which I just used, and the word *spoudaia*, meaning "serious" or "noble," which Aristotle coupled with *teleia*. Tragic action is short and continuous; it leaves no room for distraction; but why does it seem so serious and decisive and thrilling? Because this short continuous sequel is shown as involving the deepest and most important issues. In one day Medea will die, or kill. That is a fact. But also, in one day all her former love, and sacrifice and hope, will be thrown into the balance; Jason's honor will be questioned; and the rights of revenge claimed. The whole past and future will be mixed up in this special action: it is serious; it will decide; it is, in the etymological meaning of the word, a "crisis" (from *krinein*, meaning "to judge" or "to decide").

This explains why tragedy so often dwells on the past and discusses it. For all the past must be involved; and all the past must help to decide what is right and why. Let us take *Medea* again. We have spoken of urgency. But the first words take us back to the departure of the ship Argo, before Jason knew Medea: this is explanation of facts, no doubt, but it also shows how the drama came to arise, where the fault lies, and what deep resentment may have gathered in Medea's soul. The action begins on one special day; but the moral problem can be traced back years ago. And this is true not only of the prologue. All through the play, everybody will mention the past, over and over again. The two kings find in it reasons for acting as they do. Medea and Jason find in it arguments for their claims. "I shall begin first by what came first, I did save you," argues Medea (475); but never does Jason forget that she was a murderess: she had killed her brothers: "These were your beginnings," he exclaims (1336).[9] These beginnings, to which all the characters turn back, help us not only to understand their motives and actions but to see how justice and revenge, prudence and violence, are all involved in these actions.

If that is so, tragedy is not only connected with the consciousness of time in so far as it reproduces a continuous series of events, carried by the very rhythm of time: it is also connected with this consciousness in another and wider manner. For it suggests a perpetual reflection about the relation between this series of events and the past or the future; it discusses and meditates about intricate causes and responsibilities. Therefore it always presents us with a more or less conscious philosophy of time This may be another reason why we find in tragedy so many general remarks about time, and may also suggest it is no chance that tragedy was born at the same time as history.

[9] The numerals in parentheses refer to line numbers of the plays.

❖ ❖

A short, continuous, crisis, the origins and consequences of which cover a large span of time and distant connections —such seems to be the double requirement of tragedy, and its double relationship to time. But these two demands may be a little difficult to combine; and before we go any further, it may be worth while examining how in fact our three great tragedians did succeed in combining them. A history of their solutions may throw some light on the inner development of tragedy itself.

With Aeschylus, the length of time and distant connections are much the predominant feature. And they are the most surprising for us, as they are so different from our modern habits.

Indeed, in all the plays, one sees long passages where the chorus or even the heroes deal at length with events that happened sometimes one or two generations before, and, in any case, several years before. The parodos of the *Persians* thus recalls how the army left; and that of the *Agamemnon* begins with more than two hundred lines about the departure of the fleet ten years previously. These past events inspire fear; and they are dwelt upon as foreshadowing disaster, as a just reversal of fortune. But this is not all. If each play contains a crisis, each crisis, in its turn, prepares for the next one. The three plays make up a trilogy; and although we may enjoy each one as a separate work (we modern people generally have to), we cannot really understand all the implications without considering the three of them. The only trilogy that we have offers good evidence of this. For if Agamemnon's behavior and the crimes of his ancestors explain his being murdered, and explain it not only in terms of psychology and revenge, but in terms of divine justice, this very murder calls for a new revenge, which will call for another. Each play toward the end provides the theme that will be treated in the next one. Thus, toward the end of the *Agamemnon*, the chorus-leader already mentions the possibility of Orestes' coming one day to avenge his father ("unless a god guides Orestes and brings him back here . . ."); and toward the end of the *Choephoroi*, Orestes runs away, in an agony of fear, followed by the same Erinyes who will be actually present in the *Eumenides;* and the chorus then asks: "Where will ever be achieved, where be lulled and cease, the anger of Ate?" The tension in each tragedy is thus reinforced and strengthened by the presence of the others. Each action is made to bear on the whole history of the house of Atreus: the weight of the past is felt as heavier, the anxiety as more devastating, the issue as of more meaning.

But, at the same time, within each particular tragedy [10] Aeschylus is careful to lay stress on the urgency of the actual crisis; and it is easy to see how he manages to make all this heavy past crystallise around one decisive moment.

In the *Persians*, which is a tragedy of mourning, there is almost no action; yet there is expectancy, an expectancy made more urgent by a threatening dream. And as for the decisive blow afforded by the messenger's news, its critical importance shows in the following chorus-song. The first words of the introduction are "O Zeus King, now . . ."

[10] Except perhaps the *Prometheus*, where there is even less action than in the *Persians*. Yet an impression of urgency is powerfully suggested toward the end.

(532), and the same "now" recurs at the beginning of the song proper: "Now the whole land of Asia is mourning."

In the tragedies where some action is to be found, Aeschylus always succeeds in conveying a strong impression of urgency. In the *Seven against Thebes*, the very beginning of the play suggests that the decisive hour has come: "now," "now," "soon" (in line 10: *nun;* 21: *nun;* and 58–59, several words suggesting imminent events or haste). And the first scenes are full of preparations, prayers, wishes, fears—all pointing toward this one moment of exceptional importance: "When, if not now, shall we engage in prayer?" (102). Everything is worked into a sort of climax, culminating in one single deed.

The *Suppliants* shows similar structure. The play begins in an atmosphere of terrified supplication; and when the crisis arrives, its urgency is announced by all, as all say that the time has come. Again, the song sung by the chorus begins with *nun:* "Now is the time when the gods could listen" (630). Indeed, danger is approaching: "the swift-winged ships are here; there is no time left" (735).

In the *Oresteia*, it is very remarkable to see how this inner tension in each play is combined with the general connection between them. The *Agamemnon* begins at the very moment when Argos learns that Troy has been taken, when the messenger arrives, when the King comes back; [11] and we are made aware that this is the fatal moment, the crisis; we know it not only because of the chorus' obscure fright, or of Cassandra's visions, but also because Aeschylus insists on the particular moment: "Now I shall enter

[11] That these three events should follow so closely is, of course, impossible: but it is interesting to see that, precisely, Aeschylus has violated chronological likelihood in order to strengthen the climax.

the palace . . ." (851: *nun*), says the King, and Cassandra soon enters it too: "The day has come," she says. From the beginning to the end of the play, one single deed is getting nearer and nearer, through a series of steps, each one feared and watched for in increasing anxiety.

The *Choephoroi* similarly begins on the day Clytemnestra has had her foreboding dream, on the day Orestes has returned; and the action similarly tightens toward one single deed, for which everything prepares. Once more, when the time for this deed approaches, we find the same stress laid on its imminent character. When Orestes enters the palace, the chorus repeats, three times, that the crisis has come: *Nun epakouson, nun d'eparēxon, nun gar akmazei* . . . (725 ff.), and later, again we find, at the beginning of a song, the same *nun*, which recurs also when Aegisthus, after the others, enters the house of crime and revenge.

The same structure is found in the *Eumenides*, where the action grows in continuous tension until the time of the trial arrives, when everything will be judged and settled. And again, there is a stasimon, just before that moment, beginning in line 490, with the same word "now": "Now will new rules arise through revolution."

Such a structure is easy to detect, for it is extremely simple. It may even be thought of as being too simple. Indeed it requires very special circumstances. The crisis, to be thus prepared for, must be one single deed, easy to foresee. In Sophocles' plays, however, such conditions no longer existed: the action was more complex and more was left for dramatic surprise. With him, tragedy centers on one hero, whose life or fame, or whose life and fame, are in danger of being destroyed and generally are destroyed. Therefore there is no longer any necessity of including a long period of time around the tragic crises: the past life and fortune of the heroes are enough, and one single tragedy is enough to recall them, in a quite natural way. But, on the other hand, the tragic crisis is more closely tied to the hero's action: it no longer has the wide simplicity of divine justice: it varies according to man and becomes more complex and more intricate. Thus Sophocles has to change stress. And it may be of interest to see how Aeschylus' devices, with Sophocles, have been but slightly altered—just enough to become adapted to this new sort of tragic crisis.

We can see this change of stress in two items, one dealing with the oracles and preparations, the other with the urge and climax.

In Aeschylus the events could be foreseen; in Sophocles it should be noticed that oracles often foretell not what will take place, but when.[12] That is to say, they point to a crisis, while leaving its result in the dark.

In the *Trachinian Women*, this use of oracles shows from the very beginning of the play. Deianeira is worried because of an oracle that Heracles knew: "He fixed the time beforehand: when his absence would have lasted one

[12] In Aeschylus, oracles or prophetic signs never give an indication of time (except the prophecy in *Prometheus*, 774, where the time mentioned is so distant that it sounds unreal). On the contrary, the misunderstanding of prophetic signs bears on the interval of time (*Persians*, 739–741: "Alas, swift indeed has come the fulfilment of the oracles, and 'tis my son upon whom Zeus has caused their issue to descend. Yet I have been resting confident that only after a long lapse of time, the gods would in some way bring them to accomplishment" (trans. H. Weir Smyth, in the Loeb Classical Library).

year and three months, then his fate was to die, or, if he survived that limit of time, to live henceforward a life free from sorrow" (164–168). That is to say, there will be a crisis, and this crisis has come. This is why Deianeira's fear opens the tragedy, for: "This is the precise moment of time, when the fulfilment of that word is due." [13] In that way the same feeling of urgent expectation is aroused, although there is now more room for personal choice, and change, and surprise. And, as we can see, this new approach is still focused on time; only it is focused not on time's great length and continuity, but on its immediate importance when the action begins.

That this kind of oracle is familiar to Sophocles is confirmed by many examples, even when the mention of the oracle is not used for producing expectation or suspense, but only for adding a sort of solemn importance to the action at hand. This is the case in another passage of the *Trachinian Women.* Toward the end, Heracles, who is going to die, recalls the fact that long ago, in Dodona, the oracle spoke for him, and he insists on the time foretold with powerful words: "He told me that *on this very day, now alive and present*, the toils laid upon me should be brought to an end." [14] Heracles had thought this meant a happy end, whereas it meant death; again, time is what the oracle lays stress on, thus giving greater magnitude to the actual crisis.

The same device appears in the *Ajax.* That the crisis is urgent and serious is well suggested by the whole beginning of the play, where the situation is seen to be disas-

[13] The word χρόνος is used three times in the few lines quoted—not counting expressions such as τότε, τὸ λοιπὸν ἤδη, νῦν.

[14] 1169–1171: χρόνῳ τῷ ζῶντι καὶ παρόντι νῦν.

trous. Yet Sophocles has added something to make it more solemn: when Ajax has gone away and his companions think he will live and all will be well, the messenger comes with an oracle: Teiresias has told Teucer to look closely after Ajax: "He told him and conjured him to keep Ajax indoors by all means *during this very day now shining upon us* and not allow him out, if he wanted ever to see him alive." Indeed "the wrath of divine Athena will vex him *on this day alone*." And later again the messenger repeats that "it is *on this present day* that the issue will be for him either death or life." [15] Either . . . or, but now: this of course puts a strong emphasis on the impending crisis: it creates haste and panic among the hero's friends, suspense for the spectators, and makes the scene that follows stand out as decisive.[16]

The same thing recurs also in the *Oedipus at Colonus*, where we learn from the very start that the important time has come for Oedipus. He has been told clearly that on his arrival at Colonus his life would undergo a complete reversal (91). We may compare this with the oracle which, in Aeschylus, told Orestes that he would have to wander about till he should arrive in Athens, where Apollo would see to his liberation; [17] the oracle is almost the same, but in Aeschylus it is given beforehand and opens an un-

[15] The indications of time are strongly emphasized: cf. 752 ff.: *κατ' ἦμαρ τοὐμφανὲς τὸ νῦν | τόδε*; then: *τῇδε θἠμέρᾳ μόνῃ*; and again (801): *καθ' ἡμέραν | τὴν νῦν*.

[16] It will be noticed that gods, in Sophocles, are very much interested in fatidic time. In the *Philoctetes*, we see that all the hero's miseries arise from the fact that the gods would not allow him to take Troy "before the time had come when it was said that Troy was fated to fall, thanks to his shafts" (199–200: *πρὶν ὅδ' ἐξήκοι χρόνος, ᾧ λέγεται χρῆναι σφ' ὑπὸ τῶνδε δαμῆναι*).

[17] *Eumenides*, 79 ff.

determined period of expectation, while in Sophocles it is given when the time has come and when the final crisis is at last arriving.[18] But this is not enough, for, in the same play, we soon see that other oracles make it decisive to know which city will be favored with Oedipus' tomb, thus opening a conflict and a new crisis; and later again, when Oedipus is about to die, several signs and mysterious omens draw the attention of all toward the coming event.

This systematic alteration in the use of oracles is not all. And it is only natural that along with it, we should also find in Sophocles a continuous insistence on the progress of the crisis itself.[19] Only, as the action has grown more complex, its different stages are made to stand out one after the other. The ancient device of Aeschylus is now used again, but multiplied all through, in a complex system of accumulated dangers. This new complexity can be shown in two examples, which I shall choose from two different times of Sophocles' career as a dramatist.

Among the early plays, I select the *Ajax*. There, we first hear about the pathetic situation recently created: "The time has come to veil our heads," sings the chorus

[18] This impression of "at last" is conveyed by line 103: *δότε | πέρασιν ἤδη καὶ καταστροφήν τινα.*

[19] All the plays provide examples of this insistence, if not quite so striking. Sometimes we find urgency (*Phil.*, 15), sometimes paroxysm (*Trach.*, 1045–1047, 1074–1075), sometimes an impatience that gives weight to an arrival or a revelation (*Oedipus Rex*, 73, 289, 1050). In the *Electra*, we find, first, the announcement of impending punishment (478, 489), then an impression of urgency, strongly emphasized when time for action has come (1337–1338: "Delaying is wrong in such matters: this is the decisive time for having this over," *ἀπηλλάχθαι δ' ἀκμή*; 1368: "Now is the right time for action," *νῦν καιρὸς ἔρδειν*; 1389: "The dream of my soul will not remain in suspense a long time"; 1397: Hermes "will wait no more").

(246); and never has one seen Ajax in such a state (as we read in line 318: "never before"; or in line 411: "he would never . . ."). Yet hope arises: *now* one can rejoice (707: *io! io! nun au, nun* . . .). But, alas! no: the news about the oracle may have come too late (738–739). One must make haste (803: "Hurry, quickly!"; 811: "This is no time for idleness"). Even when Ajax is dead, the crisis is not at an end: will it be possible to bury him? this is a serious issue: "A terrible quarrel will be contested: as quickly as you can, Teucer, make haste!" (1163). Through good and bad fortunes, the rhythm of the crisis is kept going with renewed urgency.

The *Oedipus at Colonus*, written at the end of Sophocles' life, shows a similar method. We have already seen that the oracle at the outset drew attention to the opening crisis. But that is not all. Theseus is expected. Soon we are made to expect other and more dangerous visitors: they will come *immediately*, *in no time* (394). We are also made to expect promises from Oedipus himself (580: with time, not at the present moment"). Threats and promises have to combine, and the result will decide Oedipus' fate. Now, this twofold expectation suddenly tightens into urgency. First, the threat: it becomes a question of time, through Creon's arrival and Creon's violence.[20] So there is haste again, and words meaning "quickly" (885: *sun tachei;* 897: *hōs tachista;* 904: *sun tachei*); soon the whole song of the chorus deals with anxiety over the impending result (1057: "They will soon meet . . ."; 1074: "Has the action begun or is it going to?"). This suspense indeed

[20] Cf. 861–862: *τοῦτο νῦν πεπράξεται, ἢν μὴ*. . . . This clause suggests to the spectator a possible doubt as to the issue: it is the same doubt as the one left by the oracle.

should be enough to fill a play. But there is also the other expectation, the good one. We have seen that, there also, everything tells us, with thrilling portent, that the time has come. And, since the time has come, another haste takes place: Oedipus must speak to Theseus before he dies; and he is going to die, and does not see Theseus. He calls, he insists: "This winged thunder of Zeus will take me to Hades: send for him quickly" (*hōs tachos*); "O my daughters, the end of my life as predicted to me has come; it cannot be avoided any more"; "Let someone go, as quickly as possible, and fetch the lord of this country!"[21] Anxiety and solemnity blend with one another: "Is the man near? Will he find me still alive, children, and master of my mind?" All this because—Oedipus repeats it solemnly later—the time has come, the decisive time, *rhopē biou* (1508).

This special mixture of foreboding and uncertainty, of solemnity and urgency, is peculiar to Sophocles; it implies a combination of actions and counteractions, the success of which depends on time.

This is dramatic tragedy, tragedy as we still know it.

We still find it in Euripides—at least when there is a real crisis, prepared beforehand.[22]

Yet even in that case, there is a difference; for the impression of urgency now arises from the very need the

[21] The words suggesting haste are numerous in lines 1472–1475: ἥκει—κοὐκέτ' ἔστ' ἀποστροφή—ὡς τάχιστα.

[22] In the *Alcestis*, an early play, the crisis is presented as it might be in Sophocles. The play begins—and the text insists—on the decisive day, when the queen must die (105: κύριον ἦμαρ; 147: πεπρωμένη . . . ἡμέρα; 320: οὐκ ἐς αὔριον, | οὐδ' ἐς τρίτην μοι μηνὸς ἔρχεται κακόν, ἀλλ' αὐτίκ' . . .). Similarly, for *Medea*, see above, p. 9.

characters suffer from. There is no foreboding, no rational expectancy, almost no hope left. Still, in that very need, the decisive event happens. Thus time is still all-important, but now it presides over chronological combinations that seem due to chance.

In the *Heracles*, for instance, we have the first part of the play, where all the drama arises from the fact that the hero delays too long before returning. Will he come in time? His children inquire: "Mother . . . when will he come back?" (75); who knows? "If ever the door makes a noise, all rise up, ready to fall at their father's knee" (78–79). Meanwhile, the tyrant gets impatient: "How long will you try to keep on living?" (143: *tin' es chronon*). The victims begin to despair; everything is ready for the sacrifice: just in time, at the very last minute, Heracles appears. This was the desisive moment (532: *akmēn*). But what nobody had expected occurs soon after: Heracles becomes mad; and the recent success turns into unpredictable disaster. One part of the play is based on chronological combination; the other is not.

In the *Andromache*, the first scenes also center around passionate expectancy of a savior's arrival; and the danger becomes more and more urgent till the savior arrives, just in time.[23] But less stress is laid on the expectancy; nothing much is said about the savior till he actually arrives: Euripides lets his spectators, as well as his heroes, despair, so that the solution should be more of a surprise and "coup de

[23] In the prologue, Andromache's fear is a general one. But murder is soon planned against her son (68–69) and against herself (167). This last threat grows more and more precise. Andromache has to choose (316 ff.). She is going to be killed (425 ff.); and the time of her death approaches.

théâtre." This agrees with what we have seen of the second part of the *Heracles*. Indeed the second part of the *Andromache* also throws us into new and unforeseen reversals of fortune.

In fact, these are the twin features of Euripides' theater.

On one hand, narrow escapes and skillful timings: Will Ion kill Creüsa before he finds out she is his mother? Will Iphigeneia kill Orestes before she finds out he is her brother? Will Merope kill her son, or will she know in time? Will Hecuba and Deiphobus in the *Alexander* also kill too soon? And what about the murders stopped just in time in the *Hypsipyle* and the *Melanippe?* Time and exact timing play no smaller role in the plays including guile and deceptive plots. Iphigeneia's scheme in the *Iphigeneia in Tauris* was meant to gain time while she prepares her flight and her prisoners' escape; the text insists on the idea.[24] And Orestes' scheme in the *Orestes* rests on the exact moment of the return of Hermione—on the idea of nobody's entering the house too soon[25]—that is to say, on time.[26]

On the other hand, Euripides' plots have become so complex, so full of surprise and reversals, that the crisis finally tends to dissolve into various and independent incidents. Be it plays with stratagems and surprises (as the *Helen*) or plays with a series of tableaux (as the *Trojan*

[24] 1336: *χρόνῳ δ'ἵν' ἡμῖν δρᾶν τι δὴ δοκοῖ πλέον* . . . ; 1339: *ἐπεὶ δὲ δαρὸν ἦμεν ἥμενοι χρόνον*. . . .

[25] 1211: . . . *τίνος χρόνου*; 1215: *τοῦ γὰρ χρόνου τὸ μῆκος συντρέχει*; and see 1219.

[26] Even in small details, time is used to justify the movements of the different characters (for instance, in the *Suppliants*, Theseus arrives because his mother has been a long time away—91: *χρονίαν ἀποῦσαν ἐκ δόμων*).

Women), his last plays have almost all lost the tension of the earlier period.

In thus comparing the three great tragic authors we seem therefore to achieve a double result. First we have seen that a regular evolution goes on from one author to another—which suggests that it will be of interest to examine each one's own philosophy of time, as we shall do in the third, fourth, and fifth chapters. But also this regular evolution implies a very close connection between tragedy and time. For when Euripides stops building his plays around this tense expectation and climax, which with different emphases had been the law of Aeschylus' and Sophocles' plays, we can say we touch the end of Greek tragedy. After Euripides, and after the evolution is completed, tragedy exists no more. It dies when it frees itself from the rhythm of an action tightly clinging to time.

And yet, although time is so important a factor in the structure of tragedy, it is obvious that this structure is not wholly commanded by the urge of time, and that the invention of this literary form implies a view of time slightly different from our modern views.

It is generally admitted that ancient Greeks had more concern for permanence than for evolution. They have even been very widely credited with doctrines like cyclic time and eternal repetition. This notion has often been exaggerated; but it is true that they cherished the idea of a *cosmos*, where everything would be in order, and where time would preside over the regular alternation of things, not over an open progress or perpetual transformation.[27] Time is generally thought of as a threat, not as a continued evolution. This view easily agrees with some of the most special features of Greek tragedy.

Of course it agrees with the limited length of the crisis. And it is obvious that no Greek author would have thought of writing a play about time—as our present authors so often do, showing us young heroes in the beginning, that are old wrecks in the end; the Greeks did not like to show even the action of time on moods and feelings: when Euripides allowed one of his characters—namely Iphigeneia—to change her decision within a short time, Aristotle was shocked: apparently the Greeks were not ready for such cues as Racine's, when Hermione disowns the murder she has just ordered and exclaims: "Qui te l'a dit?"

But tragedy also retains a nonmodern notion of time in its very structure. For all we have said about continuous time and urgency in tragedy should indeed be completed by one further remark—that this very urgency breaks up, between one episode and the other, leaving room for the chorus' songs.

This division, in itself, is remarkable. It means interruption and alternation: scenes and song follow in turn, like metopes and triglyphs in a Doric frieze. And the whole acquires a sort of inner harmony, with regular pauses, just as orderly as the orderly arrangement of nights and days

[27] About the meaning of memory for the Greeks, see J. P. Vernant, in *Mythe et pensée chez les Grecs, études de psychologie historique* (Paris, 1965), pp. 51–78: the article shows that, through memory, man does not try to grasp the past, but to seize a divine and everlasting truth.

or summers and winters. In that respect this structure, which is special to Greek tragedy, can be said to agree with a notion of time where man's difficulties do not destroy the everlasting harmony of the whole.

Still more illuminating are the contents of these songs. For their purpose is sometimes to comment upon the action and heighten the impression of impending crisis, or give voice to the fears or hopes or regrets which mark its development. But not always: quite often the chorus' songs provide a kind of counterpoint to the action; they enlarge it, make it bear on deeper issues, and link it with general themes, on which to ponder and meditate; with these new themes, the pressure of time is forgotten and abolished.

This result can be achieved in several ways, among which two are worth mentioning here.

First, these songs can link together past and present events, so as to comprise a whole history with its full meaning. This is what occurs in Aeschylus, where so many songs deal with past events, because they try to find in them the seeds and explanation of what is going to occur or has just occurred. Such a preoccupation seems natural enough and might be considered as modern. But what is not modern is that past actions or dead persons not only provide a clue for understanding what rancors or obligations weigh upon the present time: these past actions or dead persons, for Aeschylus, are still alive and still active; and one can acknowledge their presence in what is actually going on. In other words, the past is not wholly past.

This accounts for the ease with which the dead come back and interfere with the living: Darius comes out of his grave in the *Persians;* Agamemnon is the center of the longest scene in the *Choephoroi*, where all gather around his grave, calling for his help.[28] In the beginning of the *Eumenides*, the Erinyes themselves are scolded and roused up by Clytemnestra's ghost. Nothing ever dies in Aeschylus. Crime surely does not: "When blood has been once drunk up by the earth that feeds us, avenging murder becomes stiff and solid; it flows away no more." [29] Vengeance is in a way an action done by the dead victim: hence the double meaning of Clytemnestra's word, when she exclaims, before dying: "I say that those who are dead are killing one who lives" (*Choephoroi*, 886). Indeed, all the plays of Aeschylus are haunted by mysterious and supernatural powers, embodying this everlasting demand laid on people by ancient crime. Dwelling upon the past is therefore dwelling upon the present: time does not count when the powers raised up by crime are once at work.

For similar reasons, the relation between past and present may be one of identity. In the *Suppliants*, for instance, the young Danaids keep returning to the history of their ancestor, Io. Naturally, this is the best of arguments for obtaining the king's help. But it should be noticed that, in their minds, both stories are one and the same: they are Io revived in her distant offspring and they hope to be saved as Io was: "Zeus! against Io is this godly wrath directed: I know this is the envy of a wife, conquering all heaven" (161 ff., repeated after 175). And therefore they pray to Zeus: "Restore anew the tale of thy kindness" (534). This justifies the long evocations of Io, or, in other plays, of other past events—which, it will be noticed, are

[28] 306–510; but one should add the first invocations by Orestes (at the beginning of the play) and Electra (130 ff.).

[29] *Cho.*, 66–67; the whole of this song deals with similar ideas.

all told in the present, a present that is, of course, historical present, used in a narration, but which is also the tense of everlasting and everliving reality. No doubt this presence is one of the features giving to Aeschylus' poetry its powerful and startling impact. With him, time is abolished under the pressure of archaic terror.

Such a trend of thought is therefore special to Aeschylus. And although similar themes may recur in Sophocles or Euripides, they do not receive there such powerful treatment as in Aeschylus. On the other hand, these two authors, especially Sophocles, provide good examples of another and more natural way of getting away from the limits of time, which is seeing in it something general and eternal.

According to this new scheme, the past can be mentioned as being of similar features as the present. This is what we find in the *Trachinian Women* and the *Antigone.*

In the *Trachinian Women,* when the fatal passion of Heracles for Iole has just been found out, the chorus sings about the ancient fight between the two lovers who used to court Deianeira, the hero's wife. This fight has something to do with one of the major characters, but it does not explain or foreshadow anything. What it does is to use an example *ad hominem* to point out the terrible influence of love, thus giving a new and more general meaning to what we have heard of Heracles' passion. Indeed, the first words are: "Great is the power making Cypris always victorious" (497): the past legend, brought into contact with the actual situation, turns it from something unique and precise into something less personal and particular; it thus releases the grip of time, and stops to consider the general idea underlying the course of events.

Similarly, in the *Antigone*, when the girl is taken away, the chorus, instead of weeping or wondering about what happens, turns toward the mythical past: "Danaë too has suffered. . . . And yet she was also, my child, of a glorious family. . . . But the power of fate is a terrible one" (944 ff.). After Danaë's woes comes the sad destiny of Lycurgus, of the sons of Phineus, and of their mother: "She was a daughter of gods; and yet on her too did the long living Fates direct their attacks, my child." That the chorus' interpretation should be wrong, when placing these punishments on the same level as Antigone's, does not really matter for us: what matters is that, at the most pathetic moment, the action is stopped, and leaves room for a series of narratives, in which the image of the last episode is repeated over and over again, as in different mirrors, thus evading the particular and freeing itself from the grip of time.[30]

But this reference to other similar legends is only the first step on the way leading to the abolition of time.[31] By far the most frequent case, in Sophocles, is the direct leap into general themes. This one can see in almost all the plays. In the *Antigone*, the discovery of the forbidden deed is closely followed by the song about man's greatness and possible folly; and the scene with Haemon finishes with a song about the power of love. In *Oedipus at Colonus*, Theseus' promise ends in praise of Athens, and when

[30] The characters may occasionally yield to a similar trend of thought: see for instance Antigone, comparing herself to Niobe (*Ant.*, 823). It will be noted that the comparison may enhance the present, for instance when the woes of Philoctetes are compared to that of Ixion (*Phil.*, 676 ff.).

[31] We have dealt with it first because it provides a good contrast with Aeschylus.

Oedipus is made to accept his son's entreaty, we have a song about the miseries of old age. That is to say, Sophocles, according to various intentions, chooses one feature or another in what has just been portrayed in the action, and treats it as general; and by doing so he completes the previous scene, endowing it with a poetic and nontemporal shadow.

This is what Euripides does on some occasions[32]—although his songs are so much shorter. Sometimes, also, it happens that the characters themselves wish to evade the urge of time, and that this sort of rest, generally provided by the chorus' songs, finds a natural explanation in a psychological disposition. Hence so many sudden flights toward something different: toward the past,[33] or toward an impossible ideal, toward previous or desired journeys in far-off countries. Under this psychological excuse, the former habit of making a pause is maintained; only it no longer invites to reflection and general ideas. From every point of view, what was most characteristic of Greek tragedy—this combination of continued urgency and spasmodic meditation on eternal themes—is giving way and declining.

This fact, however, only confirms that, as long as tragedy remained vivid, the chorus' songs retained the

[32] See for instance the song about love in the *Hippolytus*, 525 ff., the song about the heroes who died returning from Troy in the *Andromache*, 1009 ff., or the song about reasonable love, in the *Medea*, 627 ff. On the contrary, songs of Aeschylean type seldom appear in Euripides: when he mentions past events that still weigh over the present, the connection is natural and logical: thus, the judgment of Paris is a cause for the miseries of the war (*Andr.*, 274 ff.; *Hecuba*, 629 ff.).

[33] This is the case with the victims of the fall of Troy, in the *Hecuba* or the *Trojan Women*.

same function. And, in a way, this meditative aspect agrees with the nature of the general subject matter treated in tragedy. For it must be granted that myth does not really belong to any precise and determinate time. In many ways, myth is nontemporal.[34] It is a story constantly repeated, by different authors, at different times, returning, eternal, like the religious festival to which it is linked. And although it is supposed to be real (as a historical drama is), it suggests ideas of repetition and permanency.

Greek tragedy, therefore, has the privilege of accumulating, in a precarious but marvelous harmony, two opposite tendencies as regards time. And these two opposite tendencies correspond to the particular situation prevailing at the time of its birth. For tragedy arose when the Greeks had become fully conscious of the importance of time and of its problems. Yet, it arose when this consciousness was still recent, and among people who never allowed time to be the perpetual and all-pervading movement that modern authors like to declare they are caught in.[35]

From what we have seen, Greek tragedy describes an acute crisis of a temporal nature belonging to a world which, in many ways, remains nontemporal. Now we of the twentieth century have kept this notion of a crisis, and

[34] See J. Pépin, "Le temps et le mythe," in *Les Etudes philosophiques*, XVII (1962), 55–68. The author quotes Mircea Eliade's saying that myth is the negation of time; yet this should not be pressed too far, for Greek myths were about ancestors, always thought of as real, not about gods or fictitious characters.

[35] If one reads the developments about the conquests of human civilization, including those in tragedy (*Prometheus*, 436 ff.; *Antigone*, 332 ff.; and, for Euripides, *Suppliants*, 195 ff.), it is clear that these are neither chronological nor open toward the future.

our modern theater still lives on it. But the nontemporal element was to disappear progressively, as tragedy was getting further away from its origins. We have seen that the evolution had already begun in the fifth century, for the function of the chorus was fading away in Euripides. It became utterly artificial with the Romans and disappeared. Then the myth itself was to give way to historical drama (as we see so often in French classical tragedy). And finally it disappeared also, at least for a while, with the influence of romanticism.

All this suggests that Greek tragedy has a place of its own in literary history, closely corresponding to its place in the history of the idea of time. This notion will be confirmed when we see, in the next chapter, that the very words and images used by Greek dramatists when speaking about time convey an impression about time which is powerful and thrilling, but is not exactly ours.

In this field as in many others, Greek literature is of interest to us, because we see the different authors inventing the forms and ideas that we still use, and yet giving us the excitement of measuring the difference, and of understanding better how our own ideas and habits really came into being.

2 *The personification of time in Greek tragedy*

In many of the remarks about time which occur in Greek tragedy, time is spoken of as a personified being, with an action of its own; and, naturally, the particular quality of this action will be of great help when we come to describe each author's philosophy. But, before we come to that, it seems worth while considering whether the very style of all these passages does not throw some light on the Greek views about time. For time, with the Greeks, was no mythological being, inherited of old through religious or popular tradition: when the Greeks described it as a person, it was because they had some feeling about it that they could more easily convey by images than by abstract words and notions. Naturally, such images are more frequent with poets; but it should be kept in mind that the feeling need not be an original one, nor the image a new one: everything will be of interest to us, from the simple, proverbial statement to the most elaborate pieces of description, for everything will bear witness to what the

Greeks, in that period of discovery, were feeling and discovering about time.

✣

Time was not a god for the Greeks. It only became one very late and in a very special form: in hellenistic times, it was worshipped under the name *Aiōn;* but *Aiōn* then meant a sort of sacred, eternal time, which is very different from the ordinary time, or *chronos.*[1]

As regards *chronos,* nothing similar occurs. That the word is never the subject of a verb in Homer means it is not even personified. And in ancient times *chronos* had nothing to do with Kronos the son of Uranus and the father of Zeus. Indeed, confusion between eternal and ordinary time does not seem to have ever been normal in Greek thought.

When did this confusion take place, and with whom did it originate? With orphic thinkers, so we are told. But as we get this piece of information from Proclus,[2] that is to say from the fifth century after Christ, it is difficult to say how far it may be accepted as regards classical times. The various texts where the confusion arises are all too late in date to offer valid confirmation.[3] All we can say is that some orphic doctrines, of more or less esoteric nature, did, at a certain date, try to present time as a first principle, and, through an identification of names, turned it into a divine being; this goes with the fact that time certainly had

[1] Cf. E. Degani, *Αἰών da Omero ad Aristotele* (Padova, 1961), pp. 88 ff.

[2] *In Platonis Cratylum commentaria*, ed. G. Pasquali (Leipzig, 1908), 396b, fr. 68 Kern (*Orphica fragmenta*, ed. O. Kern [Berlin, 1922]).

[3] Cf. [Aristotle], *De mundo*, 401a 15; Plutarch, *De Iside*, 363d ff.

a part in orphic cosmogonies as we know them later.[4] But we are left with our difficulty.

We have, in fact, one ancient text. It is a passage by Pherecydes, that is to say from the sixth century B.C.[5] It gives Chronos as a first principle and creative divinity: "Zeus (Zâs) and Chronos always existed and so did Earth (Chthoniē)," and, as we find in one testimony, "Chronos created everything from his own seed, fire and wind and water." [6] Now this is clear and precise.

Or isn't it? I must be honest and confess that there remains a doubt. For if some of the quoters did quote the text with Chronos, i.e, Time,[7] others read Kronos, the old divinity.[8] And Hermann Fraenkel, who is no slight authority and who followed Wilamowitz, did not hesitate to say that no other text was admissible at such an early date.[9] It would certainly be impossible to discuss this question here (or the connected question of how this divine time of the orphics stood in relation to the divine time known in Iranian texts as Zervan): it is enough to see that, even if Pherecydes' text had Chronos with an *h* (as I believe it had), this was only because the author was, in a way, playing with the word, as a learned man would do, and trying to introduce new ideas under false etymologies. After all,

[4] According to Neo-Platonism, Chronos created a silver egg, which produced Phanes and Eros. But Chronos plays no part in the orphic theogony parodied in Aristophanes' *Birds*.

[5] See also Kern, frs. 54, 60, 64, 65.

[6] Damascius, *De principiis*, ed. C. A. Ruelle (Paris, 1889), 124b.

[7] Diogenes Laertius, I, 119; Damascius, *De princ.*, 124b.

[8] Hermias, *Irrisio gentilium philosophorum* (Diels, *Doxographi*, 654), 12; Probus, *Ad Vergilii Bucolica* (Keil, 1848), VI, 31.

[9] *Wege und Formen frühgriechischen Denkens* (Munich, 1955), pp. 19 ff. Those who accept the reading Chronos, often explain that this Chronos would not be exactly the abstract notion of time.

Pherecydes' date is not so ancient either. As Werner Jaeger says in his *Theology of the Early Greek Philosophers*, nothing suggests here an ancient or sacred creed, but rather the brilliant imagination of a theologian.[10] And it all looks as if some people, when the idea of time acquired more importance, had tried to force it, one way or other, into Greek mythology, where it did not belong. They bear witness to a limited effort, not to a general tradition.

Similar efforts in the sixth century B.C. were numerous. That is the period when we find, here and there, in poets and philosophers, the first personification of time. Thales speaks of time as being cleverest of all (*sophōtaton*), for he discovers everything (A 1, Diogenes Laertius, I, 35); Solon says time will show the truth (9, 1 and 2: *deixei*);[11] Theognis declares that time reveals things (967: *ekphainei*). Simonides speaks of time's teeth turning all to pieces (fr. 176). And Heraclitus, soon after, has a mysterious declaration about time being "a child playing dice—sovereignty of a child." Orphic poets thus are not the only ones to think about time, and to speak about time as a person.

So one should be prudent before tracing back to orphism all the passages in Greek literature where time is endowed with importance and majesty.

This slightly imprudent identification has been offered for several passages in Pindar.[12] And it has also been offered

[10] Pages 68–69 of the English text.

[11] See also the audacious (and contested) formula in 24, 3 (Diehl): *ἐν δίκῃ χρόνου*.

[12] Degani, *op. cit.*, p. 21, recalls the praises of Orpheus in Pindar. But Pindar is not an isolated case in that regard. At the same time, Bacchylides speaks, as would Pindar, of *πανδαμάτωρ χρόνος* (13, 204).

for tragedy [13]—particularly for the various passages where Euripides gives a sort of genealogy for time.[14] Time, he says in the *Bellerophon*, was "never engendered," but he has children. He is the father of Justice in the *Antiope* (222: "They say that Dike is the daughter of time"). He is the father of the days in the *Suppliants*,[15] and he is the father of *aiōn*, that is to say of lifetime, in the *Heraclidae*.[16] Similarly, in the *Oedipus at Colonus*, line 618, he "engenders nights and days." In most of these passages, orphic influences have been alleged.[17] If the suggestion is right (which is doubtful), the influence would indeed be neither very direct nor very profound. Apart from the fact that the words have a cosmogonic flavor about them, it is obvious that what the poet says can easily be explained in a simple, commonsense manner. It is even possible to trace, under the cosmogonic garment, the evolution and progress in the consciousness of time. For instance, in Hesiod, Day descends from Night (*Theogony*, 124 ff.); in Bacchylides, a certain day descends from Night and Chronos (7,1); and in Euripides, days descend from Chronos alone. The

[13] About Sophocles, see the discussion in J. C. Opstelten, *Sophocles and Greek Pessimism* (Amsterdam, 1952), pp. 9 ff., particularly p. 17.

[14] Already in Pindar, time is called "Father," and even "Father of all" (*Olympian*, II, 17: χρόνος ὁ πάντων πατήρ). But this is too general to sound like a genealogy: it points to the supreme power of time on all that exists (see further p. 53).

[15] 787: χρόνος παλαιὸς πατὴρ . . . ἁμερᾶν.

[16] 900: Μοῖρα. . . . Αἰών τε χρόνου παῖς. For the meaning of αἰών here, see Degani, *op. cit.*, p. 65: here it is a part of time, related to man's own experience. It is also worth mentioning that, in this passage, the reading Κρόνου was suggested for χρόνου: the late identification between Chronos and Kronos works here in an opposite manner to what we have seen before!

[17] Such suggestions find an extreme and excessive expression in R. E. Eisler, *Weltenmantel und Himmelszelt* (Munich, 1910).

phrasing is the same, but time acquires importance; and the common phrasing only makes the difference clearer. Similarly, Euripides gives *aiōn* as the child of Chronos, but Proclus, eleven centuries later, will give Chronos as the child of *aiōn:* [18] the meaning of *aiōn* has now changed and the word is used by philosophers for eternal being.[19] All these new genealogies reflect ideas, which could be expressed in more abstract language. We should say that abstract time implies continuous permanency: Euripides says time had no father. We should say that any particular length of time depends on time as a whole: he says that time is the father—father of days, or of lifetime. This is only a practical way of expressing general notions (which, as such, were recently acquiring precision) with the use of traditional formulas. It should be noted that these passages are generally to be found in the most modern and intellectual reflections, clad in figurative style.

What seems true of these short formulas about abstract genealogy may also be true of the only passage in tragedy where time appears as playing an important part in a long cosmic description. The passage here alluded to is the strange description of the universe attributed either to Euripides' *Pirithoüs* or to Critias.

What it says about time is close to what we have seen just now. As in the *Bellerophon,* time is described as not having been engendered, or, more precisely still, as "engendering himself"; [20] this is surely the best endeavor one can make to suggest, without any abstract words, the con-

[18] *In Platonis Rempublicam,* 17, 10 Kroll.

[19] See Degani, *op. cit.,* pp. 77 ff.

[20] τίκτων αὐτὸς ἑαυτόν, or, in the next fragment, αὐτοφυᾶ.

tinuity and perpetual renewal of time, which remains independent of the events themselves. But here the poet adds another image: in order to convey a stronger idea of something eternal, yet linked with perpetual change and movement, he compares time with running water, speaking of its ever-flowing stream, and using verbs of movement and life. No doubt this recalls orphic sayings about time who never grows old; [21] but, also, what better way of describing the most remarkable feature of abstract time, coinciding with change and movement, although different from them?

But this is not all. This perpetual stream, like old Oceanus, easily becomes the enveloping power that runs round the Universe. After all, when time becomes an abstract notion, when it has neither beginning nor end, when everything has to be included in it, what better way of suggesting this reality which holds everything within itself? But let us quote the description at length; it says: "Never-tiring time moves around in full and perpetual stream, engendering himself, while the two Bears, carried on by

[21] J. P. Vernant, *Mythe et pensée chez les Grecs* (Paris, 1965), pp. 69–70, writes: "Ce qui est sacralisé, c'est le temps qui ne vieillit pas, le temps immortel et impérissable chanté dans les poèmes orphiques sous le nom de Chronos agéraos. Semblable à une autre figure mythique, le fleuve *Okéanos*, qui enserre tout l'univers de son cours infatigable, *Chronos* a l'aspect d'un serpent fermé en cercle sur lui-même, d'un cycle qui, entourant et liant le monde, fait du cosmos, en dépit des apparences de multiplicités et de changement une sphère unique éternelle": cf. B. Onians, *The Origins of European Thought about the Body, the Mind, the Soul, Time and Fate* (Cambridge, Eng., 1954), pp. 250 ff. But these comparisons seem to be a little far-fetched in detail and uncertain in chronology; see also J. Defradas, in *Revue des études grecques*, LXXVII (1964), p. xvi.

the quick flapping of their wings, look after the pole of Atlas."[22] This is astronomy. And indeed the next fragment, which seems to deal also with time, adds the circular dance "which day and night, together with the stars, keep dancing along its orb." We have the stars and the signs of the Zodiac, as in ancient cosmogonies.[23] And we have the same pole, enveloping the universe, which makes us think of Aristophanes' orphic imitation.[24] Yet the general impression is of something rather elaborate, mixing together abstract notions and practical cosmology, and, anyhow, putting forward a very acute view of time's particular nature. No doubt there is an orphic flavor about it. But it may well be more orphic in tone than in tenor.

This abstract quality agrees with the alleged authors. For the lines are attributed to Euripides' *Pirithoüs* by the scholiast to Aristophanes, but many reasons tell in favor of the attribution to Critias, first suggested by Wilamowitz.[25] And Critias, the poet-philosopher, who was to be one of

[22] Fr. 594 N of Euripides, 18 of Critias (Diels).

ἀκάμας τε χρόνος περί γ' ἀενάῳ
ῥεύματι πλήρης φοιτᾷ τίκτων
αὐτὸς ἑαυτόν, δίδυμοί τ' ἄρκτοι
ταῖς ὠκυπλάνοις πτερύγων ῥιπαῖς
τὸν Ἀτλάντειον τηροῦσι πόλον.

[23] See Clements of Alexandria, V, 667. This circle does not mean that we can infer any reference to cyclic time: time brings the stars back again, but this return does not imply any repetition in the events themselves.

[24] See schol. ad Aristophanes' *Birds*, 79: *πόλον . . . τὸ περιέχον ἅπαν.* The use of the word *πόλος* in this meaning could suggest orphic influence. But the scholiast says it was the meaning with "the ancients."

[25] *Analecta Euripidea* (Berlin, 1875), p. 161. Several texts show that the attribution to Euripides was already a matter of contestation in antiquity and that Critias was already suggested as being the author. See, recently, Defradas, *op. cit.*

the thirty tyrants at the end of the fifth century, was a man well aware of all modern ideas and of the theories of Ionian scientists. Doesn't the passage sound exactly (whatever the distant influences) like the bold invention of an intellectual putting forward recent ideas? Time, becoming more abstract, is now brought into contact with the movements in the universe, which it commands and contains, although it is different both from them and from any living being. The vision is a philosopher's vision, the view a recently acquired view.

If so, we have here another proof that images about time, mythological description of time, personification of time are, in the fifth century, no religious inheritance, but, on the contrary, recent invention. Time had no traditional place in Greek myth. Perhaps it first acquired one with orphic poets. But, in Greek literature as we have it, it all seems as if every single poet, as time's importance was better appreciated, chose and worked out his own images to express his own feeling. And it seems as though these images had grown more and more precise and elaborate, from Aeschylus to Sophocles and from Sophocles to Euripides. This general impression will be confirmed when we now study two kinds of personifications, the first one dealing with time in its relation to us, the other with time in its relation to events.

Personification arises very naturally.

To begin with, let us see how this occurs. Even we moderns say that time "passes" or "approaches" or "runs away" and so on. These semi-personifications are very numerous in Greek literature as soon as one finds references to time. Pindar uses several participles implying movement: time comes or goes. It is described by the verb *herpō* ("to move along"), or by other verbs built on the same root, or by synonyms.[26] The same thing occurs in tragedy. A fragment of the first *Hippolytus* by Euripides has another compound of *herpō*, for it speaks of *chronos dierpōn* (fr. 441). We have something stronger with Sophocles: when he wants to describe Philoctetes' solitude, he says that time moved on in a slow fashion for him (*Philoctetes*, 285). Other passages will say that time "glides away" (*Eumenides*, 853) or "gathers and extends" (*Oedipus at Colonus*, 930); others (as Aeschylus, in the *Persians*, 64) that time lengthens: "Parents and wives, counting the days, quiver as they see time lengthening."[27] These semi-personifications help us to understand how the real personification takes place: the unsteady rhythm of events, the hopes and fears in our hearts, all this is transfered to a living but imprecise being, who becomes the cause of the events or who inspires the feeling. And this being is animated with the life of what he causes.

Now the personification of time as a creator of events, presiding over their arrangement, is by far the most common case, and the one which we shall deal with more at length. But the other case, although less frequent, is par-

[26] ἕρπων is used in *Nemean*, IV, 43, and *Paean*, II, 26. See also προσέρπων (*Pythian*, I, 57); ἐφέρπων (*Olympian*, VI, 97), ἐπαντέλλων (VIII, 28), ἰὼν πρόσω (X, 55).

[27] Sophocles, *Phil.*, 285: ὁ μὲν χρόνος δὴ διὰ χρόνου προὔβαινέ μοι; Aeschylus, *Eum.*, 853: οὑπιρρέων χρόνος; Sophocles, *Oed. Col.*, 930: ὁ πληθύων χρόνος; Aeschylus, *Pers.*, 64: τείνοντα χρόνον. In this last passage, the expression acquires power by the use of a rare word, ἡμερολεγδόν, which is not found again in Greek before Aristotle.

ticularly illuminating, because it helps us to see, through images and approximations, how far time was then felt as something interior, partaking of our inner life; that is to say, it provides material for historical psychology.

As a matter of fact, for this particular kind of personification, where time is shown as a living being close to us, akin to us, and mixed up in our emotions, the most numerous examples are to be found in Aeschylus.

This fact is important. For certainly, if compared with what was to be found earlier, this kind of image may be considered as the result of an evolution; and that is what H. Fraenkel and others have generally said when they explained that the powers formerly located in things had come closer to the person, had found a place in our own experience and life, and had become associated in our psychology.[28] But, if we now turn to what was to come later, to the poets following after, or, better still, to modern habits and modern views, we soon see that these images afford evidence that this was an unfinished evolution. The powers of time have indeed come nearer to man and have associated in his inner life, but they have not penetrated within him and become actually part of this inner life. Time is no longer felt as being outside, but it is not really inside either. Time lives side by side with us; it keeps an existence of its own that encroaches on ours and substitutes itself for us—as if the subject and person had not yet acquired full rights.

Needless to say, this mysterious quality thus bestowed upon time makes these images particularly startling and powerful.

The most famous example is the passage in the *Agamem-*

[28] See H. Fraenkel, *op. cit.*, pp. 13 ff.; Accame, *op. cit.*, p. 389.

non where Clytemnestra says she saw more disasters in her dreams than could happen while she was asleep—or, to translate exactly what she says, "more than the time who slept with me" (894: *tou xuneudontos chronou*). Time sleeping with the sleeper, what could it mean, if not the time when *he* is asleep? This abstract power, suddenly alive side by side with us, lives our own life. It is with us (*xun-*), and yet different.

It is easy to see the various circumstances which suggested the expression here. First, there is the general taste for images; and we have here something that can be compared to Pindar's *Pythian* 9 (23), where sleep is called "the tender bedfellow of the Virgin Cyrene." [29] There is also the fact that Aeschylus is speaking about a dream, and that, in dream, we normally experience a sort of double life, being in our bed and elsewhere, in one time and in another: still, the example shows in what fashion time could naturally become a sort of intermediate reality between what goes on within us and without.[30]

It explains therefore how Sophocles will be able to speak of time as "being with" somebody. In *Oedipus at Colonus*, he writes: "What I had to suffer and the long time living along with me (*xunōn*) teach me to accept things" (7). Jebb even translates the central phrase as "and the years in our long fellowship," thus exaggerating an image which arose naturally in Greek. Similarly, in Euripides' *Sup-*

[29] The image, here, points to Cyrene's virginity. It implies literary refinement and is very different from what we have in the *Agamemnon*.

[30] Time, with Euripides, will be our own time: the individual alone is taken into account; and if we turn to another woman with tormented nights, namely Phaedra, we see that, with her, even the reckoning of time has become subjective; and there she lies awake "in the long time of night" (*Hippolytus*, 375: νυκτὸς ἐν μακρῷ χρόνῳ).

pliants, the poet does not say, as do the translations, that a woman has been living "for a long time," but "in company of a long time" (1118: *meta*). The words have often been considered surprising, or even altered; [31] but we can see that they agree with a general trend. These faint images only repeat, in a lower style, what the *Agamemnon* had put forward with such strength—the living presence of time at our side.

If time lives at our side, it will soon borrow for itself all the transformations that are really ours. In two different passages, Aeschylus speaks about time growing old (gēraskōn), and a fragment of unknown origin also speaks of time as "getting old" (508 N). Now it must be kept in mind that, in Aeschylus, this is no external personification carried out with affected pointedness. This increasing age, borrowed by time, is ours. Indeed Prometheus declares: "There is nothing that time doesn't teach as it grows old" (981): of course, the growing old is for the one who learns, for us. And when we read in the *Eumenides:* "There is nothing that time doesn't rub out as it grows old," [32] it is to be understood that the growing old is again that of man, ultimately acquiring peace. In these two passages, time has taken our place. Was it Aeschylus' own doing or not? It has been suggested that these two passages were echoing some kind of proverb. If they are and if the words there were exactly the same (which is not sure), the light it throws on ancient psychology is just as interesting to us. For Aeschylus is here used as a mere witness.

[31] The text says: πολλοῦ τε χρόνου ζώσης μέτα δή. Instead of μέτα, various words have been offered, namely μῆκος or μέτρα (Musgrave).

[32] 286. In a fragment of Sophocles (59 N, 62 P), it is perhaps a pity to correct εἰς γῆρας χρόνου into εἰς μῆκος χρόνου.

Anyhow, and whatever the origin of the expression, time is said to grow old with us [33]—he has therefore the same age as we have, or we the same as he.[34] This is probably the meaning of the other remarkable formula which we find in the *Agamemnon*, line 107: the old men of the chorus say that at their age they can still sing convincing songs, and what inspires them is *sumphutos aiōn*. Eduard Fraenkel translates the phrase as "the age that has grown with me," but several translators just drop the idea because it sounds strange in modern languages. Indeed *aiōn* here develops along with the old men: this development is, for us, their own. Similarly, Sophocles speaks in the *Oedipus Rex* of the months that were "born with" Oedipus,[35] and in the *Ajax* of the hero's mother who "lives in (or with) an ancient day." [36] Such expressions obviously all point to a certain manner of perceiving time.[37] As a matter of fact, we can see that, almost at the same time when Aeschylus

[33] In Euripides' *Bacchae*, the poet speaks of "traditions as old as time" (201: ὁμήλικας χρόνῳ), but the meaning is different, for there, time is an objective notion and the poet means that these traditions have always existed.

[34] For this meaning of αἰών, Degani, *op. cit.*, p. 59, compares *Agamemnon*, 229: αἰῶνα παρθένειον. E. Fraenkel, who understands the passage to mean "age," says in the commentary that it is the usual meaning of "lifetime": there seems to be a slight difference.

[35] 1082. Months obviously mean time, considered in its successive elements. Also the fact that Oedipus is the son of Τύχη lends to his kinship with the months a deeper meaning. See C. Diano, "Edipo figlio della τύχη," *Dioniso*, XV (1952), pp. 56–89.

[36] 622: παλαιᾷ μὲν ἔντροφος (or σύντροφος) ἁμέρᾳ. It was Nauck who suggested σύντροφος; and it has been quite often adopted: the examples given here are in favor of it.

[37] E. Fraenkel (ad *Aga.*, 107) compares fr. 362 N, where our life "joins with us in the race" (συντρέχοι), and several phrases where πότμος or δαίμων are like sacred beings associated with the individual man.

was producing the *Oresteia*, Pindar was writing in the *Pythian* IV: "But already the old part of age is moving about me."[38] Our age is about us, close to us, with us, not in us.

After all, this is no surprise, for, in this period and in this form of poetry, all psychological forces were easily represented as having, outside us, a life which is ultimately ours. To mention only well-known examples, in the *Seven against Thebes*, cares or worries are said to be "in the neighbourhood of the heart" (288); in *Agamemnon*, fear is "in front of the heart" (976); in the *Choephoroi*, terror is "against the heart."[39] Not "in the heart," as we should say, but in the vicinity, as an independent being haunting us. And that is what Aeschylus feels it is; for he says the thing flutters and flies: he says it about fear in the *Agamemnon* (977), about impurity in the *Eumenides* (378). And these feelings can act, can speak. Even this very heart, which, in the last examples was supposed to represent the individual person as a subject, can also become independent. It can growl and jump up, sing and mourn.[40] Just as time does, it lives our life for us. And I should like to quote the expression that Carsten Høeg, the Danish scholar, used once in a private letter to me, saying that, with Aeschylus, all our feelings, and even time itself, acquired a sort of "ontological independence."[41]

This concreteness, of course, is mainly due to Aeschylus' own genius as a poet; for his images are always powerful,

[38] 157: *ἤδη με γηραιὸν μέρος ἀλικίας | ἀμφιπολεῖ.*

[39] 1024. The words are: *γείτονες . . . καρδίας*; *προστατήριον καρδίας*; *πρὸς δὲ καρδίᾳ*.

[40] For more detail, see J. de Romilly, *La crainte et l'angoisse dans le théâtre d'Eschyle*, pp. 41 ff.

[41] He wrote in French and said "autarcie ontologique."

and his world is a world where everything becomes alive with intense life. But, at the same time, it is quite clear that such poetry did agree particularly well with this period in the evolution of ideas, which marked the end of the archaic age and the beginning of the classical age. This is a special period in what Bruno Snell calls the "discovery of the mind." It is a period where all feelings were perceived in their subjective presence and yet not quite integrated into a real psychological unit. And, in that respect, the beautiful images we have just studied finally throw some light on the way in which our modern psychology was formed and transformed into what it is now.

Indeed, it is easy to see that a similar tendency shows in many more ordinary expressions, some of which have even come down to us. It certainly sounds a little strange when the old men of the *Agamemnon*, recalling the departure of the fleet, say that "time has grown old" since then.[42] It also sounds a little strange when Sophocles speaks of the time "now alive and present."[43] In these cases and in others of the same kind, we again find applied to time what really should apply to us.[44] But, on the whole, there does not seem to be anything very mysterious about these images. They could almost be kept in modern languages. And some certainly can. Do we even notice the image, when Athena, in the *Eumenides* speaks of a time to come which will be "more honored" (853)? She transfers the idea from man to time. But we still do it. And some people

[42] 983: χρόνος . . . παρήβησεν. The strength of the expression shows well when we compare Sophocles' *Ajax*, 600: παλαιὸς ἀφ'οὗ χρόνος.

[43] *Trachinian Women*, 1169: χρόνῳ τῷ ζῶντι καὶ παρόντι νῦν.

[44] Perhaps ὁ μέλλων χρόνος, in *Olympian*, X, 7, is not only "the time to come," but "the delaying time," that is to say "in which man delays."

would be rather surprised to hear that they take after Aeschylus, when they speak of "glorious times" or "singing mornings"! That similar expressions can apply to time as a whole is well known. Before I finish with this first kind of image I should like to quote some nice little lines by our Ronsard, criticizing a French expression akin to what we have seen. He says:

> "Le tems s'en va, le tems s'en va, Madame,
> Las, le tems non mais nous nous en allons."

Here is confirmation that when one tries to look for the original layers where our civilization had its roots, one soon finds many signs that ancient dispositions still remain alive, although they hide under some rationalistic and proud pretense. In the same letter which I quoted a moment ago, Carsten Høeg said he felt sure that, in an unconscious manner, time was often for him a sort of independent being—"un être *makros*, qui existe et prend couleur des événements et des états divers qu'il comporte." We still are archaic in some ways.

However, no such questions will arise with the second kind of personification. For there we shall have to deal with passages emphasizing time's power, and the approach is still ours. But the very importance of time in Greek tragedy and the poetical value of its style explain why the theme can be particularly rich.

If time is what makes the difference between two successive events and yet lasts through their succession and survives them, if it extends before and after, covering all that happened, is happening, and will happen, it is natural enough to see in it a superior being endowed with special powers and divine majesty—the more so in the ancient Greek world, which was by nature so full of gods and divine beings. In fact, time did from the start (that is to say as soon as it became a matter of thought and reflection) assume this semidivine status. It shows brightly in Pindar, where this feature has been studied a number of times.[45] But it shows with equal brightness in tragedy, where we have the added advantage of seeing how it evolved from one author to another.

This approach can be followed along two different lines: time may be considered as holding all events in stock, known and unknown; or it may be considered as accounting for what happens and as being responsible for our fate. Along both these lines, the evolution is the same. Along both, it starts with vague expressions where an imprecise being is partly personified, and leads to more precise and complete images, where the author displays literary refinement.

First, the lesser power. Even if things are supposed to exist through all eternity and to have been decided regardless of time, it is with time and in time that they come to be. He *uncovers* them. As Sophocles' Ajax says, "he makes them grow up when they were invisible and covers them up once they have appeared." [46] We find similar ideas in several passages. In fragment 280 N, 301 P, Sophocles

[45] The energetic power the word *χρόνος* acquires in Pindar has been well brought to light by Fraenkel. Among other studies see H. Gundert, *Pindar und sein Dichterberuf* (Frankfort, 1935), and D. E. Gerber, "What Time Can Do," *Transactions and Proceedings of the American Philological Association*, XCIII (1962), 30–33.

[46] 647: φύει τ' ἄδηλα καὶ φανέντα κρύπτεται.

uses the verb *anaptussein*, to unfold, display: "Time, who sees all and hears all, finally displays all"; in fragment 832 N, 918 P, he uses the verb *ekkaluptein*, to uncover: "Time, uncovering all things, brings them to light." Time is therefore the means of all discoveries and may be said to make them himself. Such is the meaning of Thales' sentence about the discoveries of time.[47] It is echoed in a passage of an unknown tragic author (509 N), where the verb is the same as in Thales: *aneuriskein.*

As time displays everything, it is a witness who brings proof for or against anyone. Already Pindar called it "the only witness for authentic truth." [48] In a more precise way, Euripides will call it by the word used for witnesses in a lawsuit: it is *mēnutēs* in the *Hippolytus* (1051). And there are many passages where it is said to reveal things. In the *Heracles*, it is said to "have shown" in full light the hero's value (805: *edeixe*). In a fragment of the *Alexander*, it "will show" who one is (60 N: *deixei*). And the image gets more and more precise. For in a fragment of the *Bellerophon*, it again "shows" men's shortcomings; but here the poet adds that it does that "by applying equal standards": [49] this is already an elaborate personification, of literary nature. We have one more elaborate still in the *Hippolytus* (430), where it is said that time "shows up" evil people "by offering them a mirror as to a young virgin." It has even been noticed that the image here implies some awkwardness, for the mirror reveals the girl to herself, whereas time reveals evil people to others. This very

[47] See below, p. 107: the personification is rather bold, but it is made easier by explanation and parallelism.

[48] *Ol.*, X, 54: ὅ τ' ἐξελέγχων μόνος ἀλάθειαν ἐτήτυμον.

[49] Fr. 303, 4 N: δικαίους ἐπάγων κανόνας.

awkwardness means that the image does not obey a strong and direct feeling: the poet develops it for the sake of literary pleasure and in order to display poetical cleverness. But in that respect, Euripides can go still further than that. Indeed, in the *Alope*, somebody was made to say: "Time will explain all to later generations, for time is talkative and speaks even without being asked." [50] This is literary personification, complete and continued in small details. It is almost farfetched. And it is Euripides.

The same will appear if we now pass on to the other aspect, and consider time as responsible for all.

If time displays things, it can, by a very natural slip, be said to cause them. It then becomes a mysterious power, half personal and half abstract, which it is easy enough to charge with the responsibility of all that happens.[51] This power stands midway between a religious and a natural explanation of things.

First, time gives birth to days, or nights and days.[52] But then how could it not give birth to the pains and joys that these days bring us? It "engenders a thousand woes" in a fragment of Euripides.[53] Thus it soon becomes a personified equivalent of fate. Indeed the evolution is so natural that it is not always easy to say where personification begins or ends. When Pindar hopes that happiness will abide

[50] Fr. 112 N: *λάλος γάρ ἐστιν οὗτος, οὐκ ἐπερωτῶσιν λέγει.*

[51] As Tournier says, commenting upon *Electra*, 781: "Le temps est souvent representé chez Sophocle comme présidant aux événements qui s'accomplissent dans son domaine."

[52] See above, p. 37.

[53] 575 N: *μακρὸς γὰρ αἰὼν μυρίους τίκτει πόνους.* This can be compared with *Oed. Col.*, 618, where we read: *μυρίας ὁ μυρίος | χρόνος τεκνοῦται νύκτας ἡμέρας τ' ἰὼν.*

for those whom he glorifies, the idea of abiding implies the action of time. He speaks of time "bringing" wealth and esteem (*Olympian,* II, 10). Now "bringing" (*agōn*) is almost abstract. But he soon prays as he would pray to a god: "May time, as it goes on, never trouble his prosperity (VI, 97); "May time, as it progressively arises, never tire doing this" (VIII, 28); "May time always govern his prosperity as it does now" (*Pythian,* I, 46); "May the great time, as it goes on, never tire being faithful to me" (*Paean,* II, 26). Even the famous passage of the second *Olympian* where time is called "father of all that is" does not do much more than emphasize a very common experience—namely the irreversible character of time. It says: "Even time, father of all things, could not make these deeds undone and not realized." [54] This power of time is, indeed, "superior to the blessed," as says fragment 33 (Snell); but even when it attains such living dignity, it remains time as we experience it in everyday life.[55]

The same ambiguous status abides in tragedy. Time is active there; its name is subject of many verbs; but what sort of time is meant? Is it the abstract notion we know? Is it a superior being? It may be either or both: time teaches lessons (*Prometheus,* 981), it rubs out (*Eumenides,* 286); it wastes away (*Ajax,* 713) it confounds (*Oedipus at Co-*

[54] One can add the way time is trusted in *Nemean,* IV, 41 ff., and also the wish of *Nemean,* VII, 67, where time is not exactly personified.

[55] Time is something one cannot evade, more than a person one must obey. Compare, in French, Ronsard, *Odes,* II, XII: "Le tems de toutes choses maistre" and, in English, the passages from Shakespeare quoted by Jebb, ad *Oed. Col.,* 610. On such expressions see the article by L. Cartney, "Father-Time," *Classical Philology,* XXIII (1928), pp. 187–188.

lonus, 609); it calms and appeases (*Alcestis*, 381 and 1085).[56] In what quality, we could not say. Even the adjectives he receives cannot tell us. Of course, when it is said to be "long" or "impossible to reckon" (*polus*, *anarithmētos*) this sounds like ordinary time. If it is called "great" (*makros*), the same interpretation is likely to be right. But what if it is called "big" (*megas*)? And what if we see it, because one cannot escape its grip, receiving all the adjectives of sovereign power, all the epithets of Zeus? It becomes "all-powerful" (*pantelēs*) in the *Choephoroi* (965), and "all-mastering" (*pankratēs*) in the *Coloneus* (609)—both these adjectives being elsewhere used for Zeus.[57]

As these examples prove, the idea of the supreme power of time did not require any oriental influence: it was natural; it was rooted in ordinary experience. For everyone wants to explain things, to imagine that somebody is responsible for what happens to us. It may be a god. But time may assume the function. And so it does in Sophocles and Euripides. As the women say in Euripides' *Suppliants* (786–788), "old time, father of the days, ought to have let me remain a virgin till now"—father, indeed as in the second *Olympian*. "Father" is what the continuity of time suggests; it is also what Zeus is generally called.

Also, we find the verb to "realize," *krainein*. To realize is what the present time does; but to realize is also the priv-

56 This is to be compared with Pindar, *Isthm.*, III, 19, where time brings in changes (αἰών . . . ἐξάλλαξεν).

57 For παντελής, see *Seven*, 118; for παγκρατής, see *Eumenides*, 918 (among other examples). In the passage of the *Choephoroi*, there is really personification, for time "enters the porch of the house" (see the quotation in note 62, below). Simonides fr. 7 (Hiller) calls Time πανδαμάτωρ; now the word applies to Zeus in the *Philoctetes*, 1467.

ilege of gods. In fact, in two fragments of Euripides, time is subject of this verb; in both cases, there are in the neighborhood similar sayings with the word "god." [58]

All this explains why editors sometimes hesitate between reading *chronos* or *theos*.[59] It also explains why ultimately we find Sophocles calling *chronos* a god. He does so in the *Electra*, saying "Time is a smooth god." [60]

Yet, all these images are unprecise. They give to time a semidivine status. They do not really suggest the image of a person, with a psychology of his own and features of his own. Where does time acquire those? One might say, in Pindar; for there is one passage where time is endowed with spatial presence and moral character; it says, in Sir Maurice Bowra's powerful translation: "For treacherous time hangs over men, and twists awry the path of life" (*Isthmian*, VIII, 14). But this time is still rather vague. It is a power more than a material being. Now let us turn to Euripides, and we find the transformation completed: time is now an individual creature, with its own shape and psychology; we see it at work, when we read in the *Heracles:* "Time is unable to save our hopes: having done his own work, he flies away" (506–507).

But the most important function of time is at the junction of the two just studied. Time is a witness, and time is a sovereign power: when these two qualities combine, he becomes a judge and the most terrible of judges.

[58] Fr. 773, 56 and 52, 8. In the first fragment, χρόνος and θεός are used in parallel sentences (θεὸς ἔδωκε, χρόνος ἔκρανε); in the other one, χρόνος is paralleled by εὐγένεια and θεός.

[59] In fragment 510 N (*adesp.*), the manuscripts have ὁ χρόνος, and Nauck writes: ὁ θεὸς scribendum suspicor. About this fragment, see below, p. 56.

[60] 179: εὐμαρὴς θεός.

Time sees all, as the sun does, but also as do Zeus and the Erinyes. No doubt that is the real meaning which tragic authors wanted to convey. Already this is what Pindar meant when he said "Time is the saviour of just men" (fr. 159, Snell). And, surely, it is the meaning we must give to the utterance in the *Oedipus Rex* (1213) when the chorus exclaims: "Time, who sees all, has found you in spite of you." It is also the meaning we must give to the lines in the *Coloneus* (1453–1454) where the chorus similarly says (but without the article before *chronos!*): "Time sees these things; he sees them always." And, once more, this threatening power can be turned into practical personification, when time becomes a person with sharp eyes or severe look. This occurs in a line I should like to be by Euripides; and perhaps it is, the origin being unknown. It says, "Time who sees all, has a sharp way of looking." [61]

The circle is closing here, for we are near the sharp teeth of time in Simonides. However, as regards tragedy, and on the whole, there seems to be an evolution. It looks as if time, for tragic poets, had first been a dim abstract presence, obscurely associating in divine action, and had progressively acquired independence. Aeschylus dealt directly with the gods, and personification of time as a supreme power is rarer with him than with Sophocles. When the gods recede further, an intermediate power is useful. But when the bond with the gods breaks up, as in Euripides, this new being loses its majesty and becomes in the end part of a literary Pantheon. This goes well with what we have seen in the beginning about the late character of its genealogies.

Anyhow, there is an amusing detail, which may be men-

[61] Fr. *adesp.* 510 N: ὀξὺ βλέπει.

tioned in order to confirm this idea: I mean the scandal raised in Athens by Euripides' mention of time's "foot."

It must be conceded that already in the *Choephoroi*, Aeschylus makes time not only arrive but cross a threshold;[62] yet the verb is in the future, and time there means the decisive time, the moment which the gods will make critical. There is a feeling of mystery and sacred epiphany, but no real personification. Not so with Euripides. For we have two passages where he speaks of time's "foot," or "step." In the *Bacchae*, the text is about the various ways in which divine justice hides "the long walk of time": (889: *daron chronou poda*). And in the *Alexander*, the poet said that "time's steps were advancing" (42 N: *chronou proubaine pous*). But this last passage is only known to us through the commentators of Aristophanes. For Aristophanes made fun of the expression. And he insisted, repeating twice the same joke and mentioning twice the same image (100 and 311 of the *Frogs*). He calls it risky or audacious[63] and puts it twice on the same level as another image which was, indeed, risky, calling Aether "the chamber of Zeus." Now it might certainly have been risky in more than one manner, but no doubt one of the reasons was that, in both cases, Euripides was offering, instead of the ancient, mysterious powers, a familiar and precise reality. Time with a mirror, talkative time, time flying away once he has done what he had to do, time's foot: all those are equally familiar images where nothing remains of the previous majesty. This majesty needed mystery. Indeed time, in Greek tragedy, only became a personal divinity when it was no longer divine.

[62] 965: τάχα δὲ παντελὴς χρόνος ἀμείψεται | πρόθυρα δωμάτων.
[63] παρακεκινδυνευμένον.

It appears therefore that this inquiry into the personification of time in Greek tragedy has a double result.

First, it helps us to understand what the problems of time can be for the mind that discovers it. Because the idea of time is already important and rich, but for many reasons still described in terms of myth, we can see how easy it is to invent a living being, who to us is the "Other," who lives our life and who causes our joys and sorrows. This invention, so powerfully brought out by the poetical genius of our three authors helps us to restore an ancient experience which is still hidden within our own, and is awakened when we read their works.

But, also, by the diversity this study shows in the way these authors proceed, and by the evolution it suggests, it invites us to look more closely at the differences. This is what we shall do next, considering more at length each author's philosophy about time and its influence.[64]

[64] For these chapters, I should like to mention the names of three of my students in Paris, Mlle Lionnet, Mlle Ruffault, and Mme Domange, who, under my direction, have studied time in Aeschylus, Sophocles, and Euripides, and whose work often helped me in getting some matters more precise.

3 Time in Aeschylus

In Aeschylus' life, the Persian wars have pride of place. He fought at Marathon, when he was a little more than thirty years old, and he fought at Salamis, being a little over forty. On both occasions, he helped to achieve victories that saved his country from invasion. Afterward he knew the years of greatness, when Athens acquired dominion over most Greek cities. It is in no way surprising that a man with such experience should be inclined to trust time. Indeed he trusted time so much that there is a famous saying attributed to him—and one that could well justify our present theme—in which he proudly declared, according to Athenaeus, that "he dedicated his work to time."[1] And, because he trusted time, he laid great stress on it in his tragedies, always showing it as bringing out justice. Time is not only with him a theme for easy remarks and moral reflections: these reflections finally join together to form a real doctrine, which, conversely, accounts for the whole structure of his plays.

[1] VIII, 347 (end).

✣

Time, for Aeschylus, is a master: it teaches a lesson (*ekdidaskei*).[2] But this lesson may be more or less severe. Its first form is the simplest and hardest: time brings out divine punishment.

Now it is quite certain that divine justice is necessarily connected with time. First, it provides an interpretation of time, the simplest of all, and, in a religious society, the most natural one: an event occurs because God has so decided, and God has so decided because of something past, that aroused his wrath. This is Aeschylus' explanation for the events described in his plays.

Once you have begun believing in divine justice, time becomes essential, for it explains the possibility of delays. Indeed, it is practically impossible to think of divine justice without having to admit that this justice is often late— and surprisingly so. This notion was a problem for many ancient thinkers, and we know that it still vexed Plutarch in his treatise *About the Delays of Divine Vengeance*. Aeschylus was not shocked; and he found there no problem. The delays of divine justice were for him natural and right.

That crime should be punished was obvious to him: "He who has done must suffer." This seems to be the law of God, and several formulas, in their hard briefness, point to the same idea; they all imply heavy, irremissible condemnations.[3] And the punishment of crime has its

[2] *Prometheus*, 981.

[3] Aeschylus says, for instance, *παθεῖν τὸν ἔρξαντα*, or: *δράσαντι παθεῖν*; see *Agamemnon*, 1560 ff., *Choephoroi*, 313–314. Also *Eumenides*, 269 ff.: *ἔχονθ' ἕκαστον τῆς δίκης ἐπάξια*.

symbol in the Erinys, that terrible divinity, whom all mortals always keep fearing, or calling attention to, in the plays of Aeschylus.[4]

Therefore, inescapable punishment.

But when? Well, later. The punishment comes "in time." Solon and Pindar had said it before Aeschylus. Solon had said that justice obliged the culprits to pay back "with time" (3, 15: *tō(i) de chronō(i)*); and Pindar had said that the proud man was to be undone by his own violence "with time" (*Pythian*, VIII, 15: *en chronō(i)*).[5] These are isolated remarks. Now Aeschylus' whole doctrine is built on that idea.

This very doctrine accounts for the fact that time is less frequently personified in Aeschylus than in the other two authors (for it does not assume what belongs to the gods), although it has more importance there than anywhere else in Greek tragedy. Indeed, with Aeschylus time is the means through which the gods achieve justice; and the idea of time is practically always mentioned in the statements about justice, with more or less emphasis.

It can be felt even in a simple but characteristic adjective—namely in the word *husteropoinos*, which Aeschylus uses twice, and which does not recur anywhere in Greek. It applies to punishment and means that "the penalty comes after." In the *Agamemnon*, Aeschylus uses it for the Erinys, and says that sooner or later the culprit is met by the *husteropoinon . . . Erinun* (58). In the *Choephoroi*

[4] The Erinys has a supreme power, and one cannot escape her. See also the lines about the irretrievable character of time (*Aga.*, 1460; *Cho.*, 48, 66; *Eum.*, 261). The gods are both witnesses and avengers (*Cho.*, 126).

[5] As a counterpart, fragment 159 (40 Puech) says that time is "the saviour of just men."

he uses it for a god-sent doom, calling to "Zeus, you who send from above the disaster for later (*husteropoinon atan*) unto the audacious and perfidious hand among mortals" (382 ff.).

Sometimes, Aechylus may insist more, and say "later in time," *husterō*(*i*) *chronō*(*i*). That is what he does in a lyric passage in the *Agamemnon:* speaking of Helen's departure with Paris, he describes divine wrath in action, and, as we read in Eduard Fraenkel's translation, "exacting account in after time, for the dishonour of the guest table and of Zeus, guardian of those who share the same hearth." [6]

Or we can have still more insistence on the course of time, as elsewhere in the *Agamemnon:* "The dark Erinyes, with the reversing course of time destroy the man who was prosperous without justice." [7]

Or we can have a whole proposition, insisting on time. In the *Agamemnon,* ancient insolence is said "to give birth, among evil men, to a new insolence, sooner or later, when the appointed day for a new birth has come." [8] Sometimes Aeschylus even insists on the fact that one never knows when justice will be achieved: this is the case in the *Choephoroi,* where it appears that for some people it is quick, and for others long-delayed, whereas there are some who seem to be forgotten.[9]

[6] 700 ff. The expression is very strong in Greek, for the words ὑστέρῳ χρόνῳ stand inbetween the two faults mentioned: τραπέζας ἀτίμωσιν ὑστέρῳ χρόνῳ καὶ Ξυνεστίου Διός.

[7] 462 ff.: χρόνῳ . . . παλιντυχεῖ τριβᾷ.

[8] 763 ff. The text is uncertain in some details. However, this new insolence is an aspect of Ate (it is mentioned just after): it misleads man in order to quicken his doom. It is fault and punishment at the same time.

[9] 61 ff. About these lines see the very good comment by P. Mazon.

Could that be a surprise to us? We know that in almost all the plays of Aeschylus punishment is made to bear on the children and grandchildren of the person who commited the evil deed. Eteocles and Polynices pay for Oedipus' malediction, which was but the result of Laius' disobedient attitude toward the gods. Agamemnon pays for Thyestes' crime, and Orestes' crime follows on the crimes of his family. A whole family, through several generations, pays one crime by another, and is held responsible for an ancestor's fault.[10]

Whoever believes in divine justice as being realized in our world has to see things from a distance and to measure time according to long series. That is what Aeschylus does. He reckons by generations and sees them in their continuity. In the *Prometheus*, he rejoices in counting by superhuman units: we hear about a savior who will come "three generations after the first ten ones" (774), and Io's future is considered down to five generations after her own son (853). Divine justice only works when considered in terms of races and generations.

But from a human point of view such belated justice creates perpetual anguish. Aeschylus' characters always seem to be held in a kind of everlasting expectancy and anxiety. Those who are in misery must wait till God's wrath is satisfied. Such is the case of Prometheus, who must suffer his torment for thousands of years, and who, at the end of the play, being thrown down into the depths, is told he will have to wait "until he has been through a great length of time." [11] Such is the case of Io, who is told she must wander about for ages ("and what you have

[10] The crime is again part of the punishment.

[11] 94: τὸν μυριετῆ | χρόνον; 1020: μακρὸν δὲ μῆκος ἐντελευτήσας χρόνου.

heard, you must take to be not yet the prelude . . .").[12] And what do the Argives do in Aulis, but wait while the absence of wind "lengthens the time over again." [13] Then they wait during ten long years, suffering repeated miseries.[14] During the same time, the watchman waits on his roof; [15] and Clytemnestra waits for revenge. Just as in the *Choephoroi*, years after, the women will be also waiting for revenge, and weeping all the time (22: *di' aiōnos*), through everlasting grief (470).

What a relief, then, when at last vengeance arrives! "It has come," exclaims Clytemnestra, "at last" (*Agamemnon*, 1388: *sun chronō(i) ge mēn*). After her own death, relief will be no smaller: "Justice has come," says the chorus, adding again "at last" (*Choephoroi* 935: *chronō(i)*). The suffering has been so long that we hear

[12] 741. This considerable length of time is also suggested by the fact that the narration is divided into several groups of lines, a new series of miseries being started with each one of them (see 705–741; 788–819).

[13] *Agamemnon*, 196: παλιμμήκη χρόνον.

[14] There is literary insistence. The messenger's speech, after the first greeting, begins with the words: "After ten years. . . ." And the monotonous length of time is suggested by the alternate succession of seasons: "And if one were to tell of the bird-killing winter . . . or the summer heat . . ." (563). The same means was used in the *Prometheus* for suggesting long miseries: "With joy, always, you will see night hiding light under its coat of stars, and then the sun making dawn's frost to melt; and yet the pain of present suffering will go on biting you" (23 ff.). See also the following note. This use of a regular succession to suggest a long waiting recurs in the famous line of Racine's *Bérénice:* "Que le jour recommence et que le jour finisse, Sans que jamais Titus puisse voir Bérénice" (Act IV, sc. v).

[15] See the characteristic lines which open the play: "Of the gods I ask deliverance from this toil, from my year-long watch, in which, lying at the house of the Atridae on my arms, dog-fashion, I have become familiar with the assembly of the stars at night, and those bright princes shining in the sky, who bring to man winter and summer."

of the "inveterate damage," or of the king's palace "lying low for too long." [16] The delays of divine action are hard for mortals to bear. In Aeschylus, they are the root of human suffering, to which they give its tragic dimension.

What is more, they are commented upon. Whether for hope or for alarm, they provide reasons for man's emotions. Sometimes, the idea of these very delays leaves a margin for hope: perhaps disaster will be delayed somewhat further? That is what Darius says in the *Persians:* "I was confident that the gods would achieve this *only after a long time*." [17] On other occasions, the same idea can help people through their long miseries by suggesting these might now end: "Fate has been *long in waiting:* it may answer our prayers," say the women in the *Choephoroi* (464–465). On the other hand, these same delays explain why one can never feel safe. The old men sing in the *Agamemnon* (983 ff.): "Time is now old, when the sand flew up with the throwing in of mooring cables, as our armed sailors were making for Ilion . . . and yet my heart within me chants, self taught, the lyreless dirge of the Erinys."

This perpetual and imprecise threat reflects the twofold nature of time. For man lives in uncertainty, and yet knows he is caught in a legitimate and unavoidable process.

He does not know what will come—never quite. And often, wise sayings allude to this ignorance. "You don't know the future," so the servants say to the imprudent girls in the *Suppliants* (1057). "He did not know the future well," so the messenger says about Xerxes in the

[16] 955: βλάβαν ἐγχρονισθεῖσαν; 963: πολὺν ἄγαν χρόνον.

[17] 741: διὰ μακροῦ χρόνου. But the oracles came true "quickly," that is to say, at the following generation.

Persians (454). "The future—when it comes, you may know about it," declare the old men in the *Agamemnon*,[18] in spite of all the oracles and prophetic signs which cause them to be frightened.

Indeed, all these mentions of an unknown future allude to an approaching doom. All are meant to suggest that one ought to be afraid. For, while men doubt and hope, the process of time is slowly maturing. All the metaphors that Aeschylus uses for the idea of time point to this maturation.

This process is already suggested by the words *telos*, "end," and *telein*, "to achieve," so frequently used by Aeschylus. Biological metaphors make it still clearer. Some of them show the development of crime as the development of life through successive generations. Crime gives birth to crime: *tiktein*, "to give birth," is used in the *Choephoroi*, line 805; *teknon* ("child"), in line 646. Crimes come back again, as accesses of a secret illness.[19] And they bring about their disastrous results, as a seed produces a plant, the form of which is already included in the seed itself. Thus we read in the *Persians:* "Insolent pride, when it comes into full bloom, produces a crop of Ate, so that one reaps a harvest of tears." [20] We find the same idea underlying several short mentions in the *Choephoroi*,

[18] 251–252. The following words receive different interpretations. In Mazon's translation, they mean: "Jusque là, qu'il aille sa route!" thus insisting on the unknown character of the future. But this meaning is criticized by Fraenkel.

[19] This seems to be the meaning of *Agamemnon*, 1479, in spite of Fraenkel.

[20] 821. The metaphor is very strongly emphasized:

ὕβρις γὰρ ἐξανθοῦσ' ἐκάρπωσε στάχυν
ἄτης, ὅθεν πάγκλαυτον ἐξαμᾷ θέρος

such as: "If we are to get salvation, from a small seed may come a huge tree" (204), or, in line 1009: "For he who waits, even the misery (of punishment) comes to blossom." In this last passage, it seems even to be half understood that punishment is all the stronger when it has been delayed—just as a tree that has been pruned develops all the more strongly.

Thus it appears that time, by the fact that it allows justice to be done, becomes a sort of positive and creative power: it brings out, in due course, the punishment which ancient deeds called for. And it really gives a meaning—their only meaning—to the various disasters which human history is made of.

But something else must be added. Otherwise time's action would be entirely destructive—destructive of sinners, no doubt, but not of these alone—destructive of generations and generations, and producing no harvest but woe.

There is one first reason why this is not the case in Aeschylus: punishment makes one think and become wiser. It has not only a practical effect, but a moral one too.

Once it has occurred, it brings both to those who have seen it and to those who have experienced it a lesson of prudence. We say in France:: "Chat échaudé craint l'eau froide"; this is a simple proverb, related to everyday experience. Well, it is very likely that Aeschylus' famous sentence, *pathei mathos*, or "one learns through suffering," was, at first, nothing more. Only, Aeschylus gave it a wider bearing and meaning. Even in his theater, it must be admitted, these lessons of time are often nothing more than lessons of prudence, brought out by experience. One "learns through evils" (*Eumenides*, 276); one learns to respect power (*Prometheus*, 10) and to obey (*Agamemnon*, 1619). But, above these practical lessons, we also find some major ones: and Aeschylus seems to think there is a great lesson in wisdom (*phronein* or *sōphronein*) brought to us by events, in so far as they display divine justice at work. This, indeed, is the meaning of the great chorus-song which opens the *Oresteia:* one remembers some cruel experience, and the pain feeds on memory; it is *mnēsipēmōn*, "remembered in pain" (180)—which means it comes with time. And "even the unwilling then becomes wise."

In fact, this lesson of experience can be brought home by a simple failure, or by other people's doom, or even by other people's failure. As long as failure or doom can be said to be legitimate, experience of them can teach wisdom. And—remarkable to say—even Zeus, in the beginnings of his sovereignty, was apt to learn through failure: in fact, the line about time "teaching all as it gets old" is applied precisely to him in the *Prometheus* (981). For time is such an essential feature of Aeschylus' world that he has to go into the evolution and history of the gods in order to grasp the final nature of justice.

But, if punishment can make wise even those who have not yet failed, there is another manner in which divine justice brings wisdom. It brings wisdom because it inspires fear. This fear of divine punishment is felt by all the characters of Aeschylus—from king Pelasgus in the *Suppliants*, inviting the city "not to nourish for later times the terrible wrath of Zeus Hikesios" (617), down to those Athenians for whom Athena establishes, at the end of the

Eumenides, instead of everlasting punishments, the existence of fear, present beforehand: "On this hill, reverence and fear, akin to one another, will restrain the citizens from committing anything unjust, whether by day or night." [21]

Thus through regret and fear people, seeing what the world is, can become wise—with time. The expression is used at the end of the *Eumenides*, when the pacified goddesses, among other benedictions, wish that the Athenians may live happy near Athena "growing wise with time" (1001). The words are quite characteristic, and the more so as they were not necessary: nothing has been said against the Athenians; they have, apparently, committed no crime,[22] experienced no punishment. Even if they had, the goddesses were powerful enough to wish them wisdom, with no specification. They say "with time," because in Aeschylus, one can only learn wisdom with time, and thanks to the lessons of time.

This lesson of time has a last consequence, which completes the doctrine and corrects some of its hardness. For if men can become wise with time, the gods can also become more indulgent and patient. I am not alluding here to the evolution of Zeus in the *Prometheus*, but to the fact that there is an end to God's wrath, always. The *Oresteia* as a whole is built on this idea. The last lines of the *Choephoroi*, after the murders of Clytemnestra and

[21] 690–692. Aeschylus insists on the idea: see later on, line 699: "Who, among mortals, will be just, if he fears nothing?"; and my book *La crainte et l'angoisse dans le théâtre d'Eschyle* (Paris, 1958).

[22] Of course, it is implied that Athens had been, or was, unreasonable in some ways. All the advice given by Athena, and the allusions to civil war, make it clear. But, even though circumstances explain the formula, the context did not require any such statement, or make it necessary.

Aegisthus, ask indeed, in awe and despair: "Whenever will be achieved, when put to an end and lulled to sleep, Ate's wrath?" [23] Now Ate's wrath does stop after the judgment of Orestes; it is, precisely, "lulled to sleep" (832); and the punishing goddesses agree to settle in Athens, henceforward acting on men only through fear.

Indeed, we find in the *Eumenides* a remarkable formula, echoing the one in the *Prometheus* which we started with. The first one said that time, as it grows old, teaches everything. This one says: "Time, as it grows old, wears out all things" (286). Now the destructive action of time is often alluded to in poetry: this will appear later on, in Sophocles and Euripides. But it will be observed that Aeschylus' remark is by no means pessimistic. It applies to Orestes' pollution; and Orestes has just said: "Blood, on my hand, is going to sleep and is being quenched: the pollution of matricide is washed out." [24] Therefore, time has brought out religious purification; it has worn out both the stain and the fault. It has destroyed (from the verb *kathaireō*, to destroy), but only what was to be destroyed; and in a way it has purified (from the verb *kathairō*, to purify).[25] This playing upon words is another example of the way in which Aeschylus turns a practical and pessimistic proverb into a religious idea and a positive creed. What is more important to us, it shows that Aeschylus can give a creative and noble twist even to

[23] 1074–1076. See also *Agamemnon*, 1337, 1479, 1484, 1535, and 1570–1576.

[24] Pollution is sometimes impossible to wash out: see *Seven*, 682, about the murder of one brother by the other: "This pollution cannot grow old." Pollution wears out when it is just that it should. As for its being worn out, with no mention of time, see *Eumenides*, 238 and 451.

[25] Some editors write καθαίρει in the text (so Stanley).

those features of time which were generally known as negative and disheartening. Indeed, time with Aeschylus does not wear out faith, or happiness, or patience,[26] but only divine anger, when it is legitimate that it should abate.

It appears, therefore, that the whole doctrine is unusually firm and systematic, and that it is central in Aeschylus' thought. It is only natural that this should show up in the literary structure of the plays. And it does more than that, for it provides the very frame according to which they are built.

Aeschylus, thinking that divine justice was always at work and extended its action over generations and generations, could not deal with any event without considering not only what came before but what came long before, even before the hero was born. For that reason, he could not confine his subject matter within the narrow bonds of one short action.

The first result of that situation was that he always wrote trilogies—not one play, but three plays bearing on the same theme—which allowed him more room to develop a whole sequel of recurrent crimes, that could be distant in time, and yet closely tied with one another by an inward necessity. The *Oresteia*, which is the only trilogy preserved, is naturally the best proof of this. But the *Seven against Thebes* could be just as good an exam-

[26] Only once do we hear in Aeschylus of something destroyed by time: it is the color of the veil, destroyed by "blood and time": even there, time is not the only, nor the first, cause of destruction.

ple, with its three titles in eloquent order: *Laius*, *Oedipus*, *Seven against Thebes:* the father, his son, and the sons of his son. And it is easy to see how heavily Laius' own fault weighs on the action of the *Seven against Thebes*, that is to say of the last play of the trilogy. For, in the middle of this tragedy, the chorus turns toward that ancient fault, "when Laius, in spite of a thrice repeated order from Apollo" (745), did what he did.

But even a trilogy is not always enough. For if the trilogy to which the *Seven* belong began with this first and fatal crime, the *Oresteia* does not begin with Atreus and Thyestes: it begins only with Agamemnon. The series of crimes here is too long even for a trilogy. And it should be added that, should the trilogy cover the whole range of events, it would still be necessary to clarify the relation between old ones and recent ones.

Hence the necessity, in Aeschylean drama, of long comments about the past.

These are mainly attributed to the chorus, whose members are not so busy with the action as the characters must be, and are generally old enough to have acquired a keen insight into the working of human destiny. Almost all the main *stasima* in Aeschylus deal more or less completely with the past. They look back to it in order to understand the present; they trace responsibilities, and develop reasons for fright.

The result is, of course, a perpetual oscillation in these plays between past and present. But this oscillation is not just haphazard and disorderly. Indeed, if we look a little more closely into the structure of the different plays, it emerges that, quite often, Aeschylus keeps for the center of his play the most distant "flashback," as we should say now, and joins it there with an anticipation and prediction about future events. So that the whole sequence of events stands there in the middle, as one great unity, where time's continuous course is gathered into a legible pattern.

It is remarkable to see that this is what occurs even in the *Persians*. Though the tragedy is what would now be called a historical play, and though Athens should normally be designated as the power responsible for Xerxes' disaster, Aeschylus the Athenian insists on tracing this responsibility to Xerxes' religious faults, and links these faults with more ancient facts concerning his family. Hence the dwelling on the past. When the play begins, both the chorus and Atossa, in turn, comment upon the mistakes or sins which marked Xerxes' departure for Greece: remembrance of past deeds and fear of future events thus follow in an alternate succession.[27] But in the very middle of the play, between the news of the defeat and Xerxes' own return, this tendency to look back to the past in order to understand the present materializes in the actual appearance of Darius' ghost, who comes back from among the dead in order to give explanation and advice. In the explanations he gives he insists, no doubt, on Xerxes' young folly; but he also points to an oracle, which he knew beforehand, though he hoped it would not be so quickly fulfilled; and he traces a brief history, starting as early as the beginning of sovereignty for the Medes, five generations before himself (765 ff.)—a long com-

[27] The old men of the chorus are afraid because of the insolence of Xerxes' departure, and Atossa is frightened because of the symbols in her dreams. Both express fear and anguish. It is worth noticing that, in the play, a relation between past and future is often commented upon: see 525–526 and 598–599.

ment about a distant past. And closely linked with it comes the prediction: Darius reveals that this disaster, which arose from folly, is not over yet: "That is why, having committed wrong actions, they suffer no smaller pains, and others are yet to come, for their woes are not yet contained, but continue to gush forth. . . . Heaps of corpses, until the third generation, will be for the eyes of men, mute testimony shouting that mortals should not have thoughts above their condition" (813–820). Eight generations are there brought together, in a long but clear causation, linking fault and retribution; and the connection is only made clear with the aid of someone endowed with superhuman insight.

If we take the mythical tragedies, this recurs in almost all of them. No doubt the *Suppliants* does not provide such a neat causation, but the way in which Io's adventures are perpetually dwelt upon is, all the same, quite remarkable. Io is the suppliants' ancestor. This kinship is their best argument, both toward the Argives and toward Zeus. It is also a sort of explanation, in so far as Io's fate is the remote model which their own adventure imitates and continues. This shows in all the first songs and dialogues;[28] and it has pride of place in the great invocation to Zeus, just in the middle of the play. There the second strophe begins, in line 538, with the word *palaion* ("ancient"): "The ancient traces did I follow, traces of my mother, who was looked upon as she had her pasture among flowers . . . "; these words begin a long reminiscence of some fifty lines, dealing with Io.

In the *Prometheus*, the causation, once more, is not very

[28] See particularly 162: "O Zeus, this is wrath from the gods, directed against Io: I know it for the jealousy of a wife, triumphing in the sky."

clear, because divine wrath is not yet divine justice. But we find similar flashbacks and prophecies—they are particularly clear in the case of Io. As for Prometheus, there is certainly insistence on his past crimes and services, and, toward the end, evocation of his future liberation. But these are too closely connected to his present fate to be surprising. On the contrary, Io's past sufferings and future destiny are narrated with full details, in a manner that is undeniably strange. Io's episode is just in the middle of the play. For this episode, the Titan turns into a seer: when Io herself has told the origins of her miseries, he reveals quite at length what she will suffer in the future, till she is finally saved, giving birth to a child whose offspring will be Prometheus' own savior "three generations after the first ten ones" (774). But the Titan does not do that alone: he also goes back to Io's first pains and travels, thus "prophesying the past," as Epimenides would have said; [29] and, after a long narration of these past events, he reaches again the future, with her salvation and Zeus' final doom. Therefore we again have here, in the middle of the play, this great oscillation between past and future, which sheds full light on a huge and clear pattern, covering several generations—the actual crisis acquiring its meaning only in this vast perspective, which lies open to us just before the peripeteia. Prometheus' drama and Io's woes are there seen as part of a whole, which extends from Kronos' malediction to a distant end where justice is victorious.

In the *Seven against Thebes*, this very peculiar structure is even clearer. For the whole beginning of the play deals

[29] Aristotle, *Rhetoric*, III 1418a.

with present things, and has about it an atmosphere of urgency; but, suddenly, at the very minute when Eteocles decides to go and fight his brother Polynices, the present seems to open before us, and lets us see in the distance a more remote cause at work. Eteocles himself announces his decision by a sudden exclamation, recalling the doom attached to the whole family of Oedipus: "O you, demented and hated by the gods, O miserable race of Oedipus, my race, alas, the malediction of my father now comes true" (654 ff.). And the chorus-song that follows (which is placed between Eteocles' decision and the news of the double death) is entirely devoted to the long series of disasters which started with Laius' disobedience. Indeed, the second antistrophe begins with the word *palaigenē*, or "anciently born": "I speak of the ancient fault, soon punished, but enduring till the third generation, when Laius. . . . " The structure is exactly what we could expect. No doubt the prediction about the future is lacking; and yet, even these simple women, unable to foretell anything, are made to fear not only the death of the two princes but the possible fall of Thebes in later times: "The oracles' edge does not wear out" (845).

Before passing to more intricate structures, let us add that the pattern of the *Choephoroi* is exactly similar to what we have just seen. The action there is entirely commanded by the memory of Agamemnon's murder, which gods and men alike wish to see avenged. But in the middle of the play, after the recognition between Orestes and Electra, and before Clytemnestra's murder, there is something more peculiar: a whole scene of invocation addressed to Agamemnon in his grave.[30] The aim is to obtain his help; to achieve this, all the details of the murder are recalled at length—both for him and for us—so that the whole weight of the past is made to bear on what will take place. As soon as that is over, Aeschylus introduces a comment about Clytemnestra's dream, which foretells the immediate future. That is to say, once more, distant memories and future prophecies join together, in the very center of the play. And, finally, it can be added that the very conclusion of the play goes back even further, pointing to the crime against Thyestes, which had been designated as the primal cause in the *Agamemnon*.

No play is more illuminating, for the function of time and for literary structure, than the *Agamemnon*. Three reasons may be suggested. The *Agamemnon* is the first play of a trilogy, and the poet has to connect his drama with events that have no place there—the more so as the trilogy does not begin with the first crime of the family. The weight of the past, also, is more complex here, as two opposite events have to be explained: Agamemnon's victory over Troy, and Agamemnon's murder—that is to say, we must hear of two different kinds of crimes. And ultimately it may be surmised that the *Oresteia*, being a work of the last years of Aeschylus' career, implies therefore a wider and more complex theory.

The result is that the play is long (it has almost 1,700 lines), but has no more than about 300 lines dealing with

[30] This could have been the subject matter for a chorus-song. The fact that the chorus joins with the characters in a long commos corresponds to the fact that the past, here, plays an immediate part in the action.

the present time. All the rest of the play describes the past—whether narrations of the war (as in the scene with the messenger) or memories of previous events (as in most chorus-songs).

In fact, it can be said that all chorus-songs, till the murder of Agamemnon, deal with the past. And with what, in the past? The first one, the vast parodos which is the longest lyric passage in all Greek tragedy, is entirely devoted to the departure of the expedition. The first words of the anapaests are "Ten years ago . . . " (40); then, the song proper describes the threatening auspices under which the troops assembled and the monstrous sacrifice which Agamemnon achieved, killing his daughter Iphigeneia. All this long narration centers round an invocation to Zeus, god of justice; and it breathes fear for the king, whom so many prophetic signs were condemning for his daughter's murder.[31]

But before Agamemnon's doom comes his success. And this success has its causes in another fault, in somebody else's fault—namely Paris' fault and the rape of Helen. That is why the two following songs of the chorus deal with this more distant crime. The first is devoted to Paris, the second to Helen. In both cases great stress is laid upon the idea of divine justice; indeed, it is clearly and majestically declared, and repeated over and over again. Now this, of course, explains the Trojan disaster; but, by a remarkable twist of composition, Aeschylus has succeeded in making these two songs, and particularly the

[31] The presage in 131 is vague and conditional; the one in 150 ff. is quite precise, and it is made sure by the sacrifice of Iphigeneia.

first one,[32] begin with Paris' fault but end with Agamemnon's. Paris' fault has brought the war; the war and its miseries are Agamemnon's doing: he ordained this war, where so many men died "for another man's wife," and "resentful grief grows against the Atridae, principals in this suit" (450). We have, at the same time, a more distant flashback than before, showing the Trojan fault, and a new fault for Agamemnon, making his case still worse.[33]

But then, one could object, is there no flashback into a more distant past? Is there no mention of Atreus' crime of obliging his brother Thyestes to eat his own children? Of course there is. We should expect it to be right in the middle of the play, just before Agamemnon's death; and there it is. Only these distant crimes are not mentioned in a chorus-song, but in Cassandra's scene. As in the *Persians* and in the *Prometheus*, we have a real prophet—one who is entitled to explain both the past and the future. More: we have here a prophet with visions, who actually sees, all at the same time, all together, in one single perception, the whole time fused into one. For Cassandra immediately sees the palace as stained with blood of ancient crimes; the palace is "a slaughter-place for man, a place where the ground is sprinkled"; and she adds: "Here are the babes crying because of their slaughter and their roasted flesh, that their father devoured." [34] This crime had been committed by Agamemnon's father. But in the same anguish

[32] In the second one, nothing is said of Agamemnon, but the stress on divine justice is most threatening.

[33] His faults in victory are stressed in the dialogue, particularly those committed against the altars of the gods: see 525 in connection with 337, and 783 in connection with 472.

[34] 1100 ff.; I quote Fraenkel's translation for this whole scene.

Cassandra goes on:" O horror, what new grief is here? A mighty evil is being plotted here in the house, unbearable to kinsmen and friends, beyond cure; and help stands far aloof." This plotted murder is Agamemnon's murder. She actually sees it: the bath, the hand that strikes; she sees it all before it happens. And she also sees her own death. Aeschylus could not find a more powerful or startling way to suggest that these crimes were but one with Atreus' crime. Indeed, he goes even farther than that. For there, in the center of the play, he joins to this distant past a prophecy about the next generation—when Cassandra declares: "Yet our death shall not be unavenged by the gods; for there shall come another to avenge us, the offspring that slays his mother, he who exacts atonement for his father. An exile and a wanderer, a stranger to this land, he shall return. . . ." [35] Atreus, Agamemnon, Orestes: the three generations suddenly stand before our eyes as one. Then she enters the palace, and the actual murder takes place.

This is enough to show that all the magnificent structure of the *Agamemnon* becomes clear as soon as it is considered in the light of Aeschylus' ideas about time and divine justice. But there is still something more to be said about it. For the play does not end with the king's murder. Nor do the mentions of the past stop there. Only, after the murder, we find them no longer in the chorus-songs, but in the murderer's explanations.

The sacrifice of Iphigeneia and the daimon attached to the house are Clytemnestra's excuses. They come first,

[35] 1279 ff. See also 1317 ff. about the time when, she says, "for me, the woman, a woman dies, and for the ill-mated man, there falls a man."

and the murder of Iphigeneia is mentioned several times.[36] Atreus' crime, on the other hand, is Aegisthus' excuse; for he is Thyestes' son. And, just as in the first part of the play, this most distant flashback comes in last—in lines 1583 and following.[37] The whole range of causes, which were developed at length in the first part of the play, where they gave birth to fear, is here taken again and repeated, in a shorter manner, so as to provide arguments. This means we actually see in the *Agamemnon* divine justice announcing human justice and making a place for it, just as we see the search for the causes of punishment leading the way toward the judiciary discussion about the legitimacy of punishment. In that respect, the *Agamemnon* prepares for the *Eumenides*, and further on for the plays of Euripides, with past actions discussed in parallel debates.

By a strange reversal of things, it thus appears that what was a right explanation, when recorded by the faithful old men of the chorus, frightened for their king, becomes a rather poor excuse, when put forward by the murderers. For revenge may achieve justice through crime and Agamemnon's death may be deserved, without his murderers being thereby justified.

However, one thing is sure: it is that these developments about the past—these flashbacks, as we have called them—are neither sheer ornaments nor the result of hap-

[36] 1415 ff., 1525 ff., 1551 ff.

[37] "For Atreus, being king in this land, this man's father, dealt thus with Thyestes, my father." Here comes at last a whole narration of this ancient crime. It occupies about thirty lines on end—and this, less than a hundred lines before the actual end of the play. Even this simple fact would be enough to show the importance of the past in the structure of Aeschylus' play, and the originality it thus acquires.

hazard inspiration. The range of facts they deal with, their order, their place—all are determined by a subtle and precise art, closely connected with Aeschylus' doctrine about time: it always illustrates one and the same idea, which controls every detail and shows how past crimes account for present and future woes.

This doctrine and this particular structure, which all the tragedies display, belong strictly to Aeschylus, and to nobody else. Yet it may be amusing to observe that a similar problem has arisen in other literary forms and given birth to solutions which, in some respects, can be compared to those in Aeschylus: I am thinking of Thucydides. For Thucydides also had to deal with a very precise crisis, which he wanted to follow from beginning to end, with a strong feeling of historical continuity.[38] Yet, Thucydides also was well aware that, sometimes, far-distant causes had to be considered and made it necessary to comment about the past. Instead of grouping these comments at the beginning of his work, as any modern historian would have done, he has chosen to do what Aeschylus did—namely, start with his historical continuity and insert long parentheses about the past, when the influence of the past was most decisive. This shows in the rather strange structure of Book I. There, he not only relates the incidents and immediate reasons explaining how the Pelopon-

[38] It is well known that Thucydides wanted to give his history a strictly chronological continuity, even to the point of dropping everything that was even slightly distinct from his main theme. It is also well known that he regarded events as making a long and regular progress (see, for instance, his views about early times, in Book I).

nesian War began but gives, more or less abridged, a short view of the history of Greece in previous times. After having stated the importance of his own war, he goes on proving this by a summary of ancient life and ancient wars. Then he begins his narrative; but, finding on his way the importance of Athenian imperialism, he again stops the narration with another long parenthesis expounding the growth of Athens' empire during the fifty years that followed the Persian wars. Other discussions similarly bring out other digressions, dealing not only with Cylon, but with Pausanias and Themistocles. That is to say we can find there a brief discourse on many things of the past, but divided into several groups, according to the different features which, in the narration, require explanation. No doubt this broken manner of exposition may have something to do with the conditions under which the work was written, and with possible additions. But a modern writer would never have disposed them like that, even if he had made additions. And I think we can trace in this particular disposition the same inner contradiction that we found in Aeschylus between a limited subject matter and a wish to explain things by looking back to more and more remote causes. The same device has been used by both, at the cost of chronological continuity, because the past was equally important to both.

This very similitude enhances the difference. Thucydides never looks for other causes than logical and human ones; and the past only weighs on the present in so far as it creates a practical situation that controls present decisions. Aeschylus' causes, on the contrary, are religious and moral; and the past weighs on the present because gods become angry with a family for its past crimes, and punish its members with continued woe.[39] One doctrine is wholly different from the other; and between the two of them an intellectual revolution has taken place, changing the sensibility of people, and giving to this weight of the past a wholly different meaning.

This final contrast with Thucydides suggests that, in a way, Aeschylus' approach is connected with the habits of his time. And so it is. It does not mean, of course, that his ideas were shared by all his contemporaries. They are far too deep and systematic, too extreme, to allow for such a supposition; and his very insistence, which suggests original interpretation, would be enough to dismiss the notion. Only such ideas could not have taken form or life in a less religious period, in a more rationalistic atmosphere. The fact is that, with the change of habits, we shall see the other two dramatists evolving new ideas and disclosing a new philosophy of time. No doubt the old Aeschylean themes will recur, now and then, in their tragedies. But these themes will have lost their inner power: either Sophocles and Euripides will repeat them by and by, with no great conviction, as a commonplace tradition;[40] or they will transform them, and, by a slight shift of emphasis, it will emerge that each of them has finally replaced the old creed

[39] There are human causes, in Aeschylus, besides the divine ones: Clytemnestra avenges Iphigeneia's death, and her feelings are easy to understand from a human point of view; similarly, Orestes avenges his father's murder; and so on. Yet, these psychological causes provide but a superficial explanation. And Aeschylus, who is always very careful to point out divine causes, is not always careful about human ones: Eteocles provides the best proof of such neglect.

[40] For such cases, see below, Chapter 4, n. 1, and Chapter 5, n. 7.

by a new philosophy, agreeing better with his own nature and his epoch.

Thus it turns out that tragedy is a good mirror. For although each author has his own personal philosophy and each play is freely invented, the history of tragedy implies an inner dialectic, in which the idea of time undergoes a steady evolution, according to the atmosphere in which it is considered—the good dramatist being the author who finds a tragic pattern suiting this new philosophy. By chance, also, they were three—which is an ideal number for dialectics!

4 Time in Sophocles

There is exactly one generation between Aeschylus and Sophocles; Aeschylus, aged forty-five, was among the fighters in the battle of Salamis, while Sophocles, aged fifteen or sixteen, was among the boys chosen to dance at the festival celebrating the victory. Therefore, when Sophocles wrote his first tragedies, Athens' power was already wide and firm. And in the pride and ease of self-achievement, people might easily be led to lay less stress on God's designs, and more on their own fate and merits. The age of Sophocles is the age of man.

This change shows in a very striking manner in the idea of time which his plays convey. Aeschylus' tragic pattern may still be found in them, but it assumes now a different meaning, and often leaves room for a new philosophy, in which man comes first. In this philosophy, the misery of man comes from the mutability of things, and his greatness from the way in which he answers it. Events, instead of being explained through some universal rule, are being commented upon as a sort of challenge for human characters. That is to say, the philosophy here is widely opposed to what it was in Aeschylus, even though it often borrows from the same stock of ideas and traditional remarks.

The difference will appear both in the manner in which the influence of time is now described, and in the fact that we shall here have to add another topic, dealing with the way in which man reacts to this influence.

✣

Time, now, is not the means of justice, but the cause of unsteadiness and lability in human life.

Sophocles, of course, knew about divine justice, and about suffering caused by ancient faults. Yet he seldom insists on the idea.[1] He does not say that the event which comes and destroys man arises from a just or unjust power: he just says that it was God's will.[2] And the consequence is that the long delays of divine justice are less dwelt upon than the sudden intrusions of God's will in human life.[3] Even when punishment is mentioned, we find, instead of an impending threat, quickness and contrast.

In the *Antigone*, the chorus which sings about the man who is a prey to Ate says: "And only for the briefest time

[1] We find it in *Antigone*, 593 ff., 856, 1350 ff.; but these are isolated remarks, not borne out by the general trend of the play.

[2] Hence the numerous discussions, among commentators, about the characters' possible guilt. See recently E. R. Dodds, "On Misunderstanding the *Oedipus Rex*," *Greece and Rome*, XIII (1966), 37–49.

[3] These delays are mentioned, but with regret: their result is that people are not made more prudent by what they see: so in *Electra*, 1505–1506, and *Oedipus Col.*, 1536–1537 (where familiarity with Aeschylus has led Mazon to misunderstand the text, not taking the particles into account, and missing thereby the change in emphasis from one poet to the other).

does he live free of woe."[4] Later in the same play, Teiresias says the same thing to Creon: "No long delay of time will take place before one hears men and women wailing in the house" (1078). In the *Ajax*, Athena herself declares: "A day can humble all human things, and a day can lift them up." And, in a passage of a lost tragedy, the *Tyndareus*, we read similar words: "In a brief and small time, the gift of a hostile fate destroys the richest prosperity, when change takes place and the gods wish it."[5]

Thus, through a slight shift in emphasis, the whole meaning changes: the stress is laid not on god and justice, but on man and change.[6] Time is no longer a coherent sequence, in which we painfully achieve the designs of transcendent justice: it becomes a series of rough, startling changes, which may occur in any manner, affecting both people's fortunes and their feelings.

The action on their fortunes is of course the most obvious.

The idea that no one should hope for continued happiness is a well-known theme in Greek poetry. In Sophocles it has received the most magnificent wording. It has indeed inspired a very famous song at the beginning of the *Trachinian Women*. One should like to quote it all; but two passages at least bear directly on time. The chorus sings

[4] 625: *ὀλίγιστον χρόνον*. In this chapter, I have made great use of Jebb's translations, introducing only some small changes, either to make the passages sound a little less archaic, or to make them more exact as regards the present theme. But the general merits are his.

[5] 588 N, 646 P: *ἐν γὰρ βραχεῖ . . . κὠλίγῳ χρόνῳ*.

[6] See J. C. Opstelten, *Sophocles and Greek Pessimism* (Amsterdam, 1952), p. 65: "Our poet is more concerned in the reaction of his heroes to their suffering, than in the cause of it."

about Heracles, and says: "As one may see billow after billow driven over the wide deep by the tireless south wind or the north, so the trouble of his life, stormy as the Cretan sea, now whirls back the Cadmaean hero, now lifts him to honor. . . . Remember that the son of Cronus himself, the all-disposing king, has not appointed a painless lot for mortals. Sorrow and joy come round to all, as the Bear moves in his circling paths. Even the starry night does not abide with men, nor does tribulation, nor wealth; in a moment it is gone from us, and another man gets his turn of gladness, and of bereavement" (114–116, 126–135).

In this small extract—or I should say, in these two small extracts—the theory of time's altering action is put forward with two different images, which might seem to suggest very different ideas. One is an image of disorder (the tempest), the other of regular and cyclic movement (the stars). But this must not surprise us. For, if the stars' movement is in itself cyclic and regular, seen from the point of view of man it means change and nothing else.

The star is now here, next there, and later here again. It is over us, then over somebody else. The world can be orderly, and yet provide the experience of perpetual loss and modification. Now it is a fact that Sophocles has been deeply impressed by this feeling. And similar images recur quite often in his plays. Even the song just quoted could offer other instances—for it begins with the alternate succession of day and night: "You whom Night brings forth when she is despoiled of her starry crown, and lays to rest in your splendor, tell me, I pray you, O Sun-god. . . ." [7] In

[7] *Trachinian Women*, 94 ff. The lines suggest alternacy even through the very movement of the words and their perfect chiasmus: νὺξ ἐναριζομένα τίκτει κατευνάζει τε φλογιζόμενον, Ἅλιον.

an equally important passage, which will have to be considered later, in which Ajax dwells upon human frailty, the cyclic succession is mentioned as an argument for yielding to others;[8] and we find there first winter and summer, then night and day: "Thus it is that the snowy winter gives place to fruitful summer; and thus night's weary round makes room for day with her white steeds coming to kindle light" (670 ff.). Indeed, the passage goes on with tempest and calm, sleep and wakefulness: "And the breath of dreadful winds can allow the groaning sea to slumber; and, like all others, almighty Sleep lets one free, after having bound him: it does not hold people for ever." Things may come back, with the revolving time: so we read in the *Oedipus Rex* (156). The days and nights succeed, according to a general rhythm: so in the *Electra* (1364), and other passages, all using the verb *kuklein* (to "go in circles") to express the same idea as regards our own fate, or indeed, all things. This *kyklos* of nature,[9] this perpetual sharing and succession in the universe does not in the least mean what we now call (speaking of the Greeks!) "cyclic time": it means a continuous movement of all things, which may be controlled by regular laws, and yet illustrate the perpetual modification of the world we live in.

This is the reason why it can be coupled, in the passage in the *Trachinian Women*, with the image of the

[8] Its function is the same in the famous passage of Euripides' *Phoenician Women*, when Jocasta tells her son that he should share with his brother, as sun and night share power (543–546).

[9] *Oedipus Rex*, 156: περιτελλομέναις ὥραις; *Electra*, 1364: πολλαὶ κυκλοῦνται νύκτες ἡμεραί τ' ἴσαι; fr. 787, 2 N, 871 P: τροχῷ κυκλεῖται; fr. 575 P: τρόχου δίκην . . . κυκλεῖ τύχη. The word κυκλοῦσιν was already used in the passage quoted above, *Trach.*, 129.

tempest at sea. This image also recurs in several plays. Sophocles has used it in order to suggest both the disorders of life and the valiance of man, who faces it all like a warrior attacked on every side.[10] From this point of view, the best example is probably the one we find in the *Oedipus at Colonus:* "As some cape that fronts the North is lashed on every side by the waves of winter, so he also is fiercely lashed by the dread troubles that break on him like billows, some from the setting of the sun, some from the rising, some in the region of the moon-tide beam, some from the gloomy hills of the North" (1245 ff.). Such a passage, to which others could be added, of no less majesty,[11] confirms that the ideas in the great song of the *Trachinian Women* were something which touched Sophocles deeply, and for which he was ready to use all the poetical devices he could think of. Indeed all the movements of nature, whether orderly or disorderly, combine together in order to enhance the frailty of human things and the challenge which man's enduring powers are submitted to.

This view is very different from Aeschylus'. For the

[10] One can compare the *Iliad*, XV, 618–622 (and see C. M. Bowra, *Sophoclean Tragedy* [Oxford, 1944]). Aeschylus also knew well about "a sea of troubles"; and Shakespeare's image is used by him in the *Persians*, 433, and the *Prometheus*, 746. But the image is never fully expounded as a sign of the unsteadiness of life, as it is in Sophocles.

[11] In *Antigone*, 582 ff., there is a passage the beginning of which takes after Aeschylus, for it speaks about the gods shaking a house with Ate; but it goes on in a less Aeschylean manner, using the image to suggest unpredictable disorder and misery: "Just as we see, when the surge is driven over the darkness of the deep by the fierce breath of Thracian sea-winds, that it rolls up the black sands from the depths, and there is a sullen roar from the windy headlands that face the blows of the storm. . . ."

change which is considered here, and the frailty it disproves, are no longer the result of one special decision of God's: they seem to be rooted in the very nature of things; they are part of man's condition; they are the features of time.

This idea is confirmed by all the passages in Sophocles that deal with time. They could all echo the song of the *Trachinian Women;* they all show the action of time in the same light.

Two of them stand apart, as insisting particularly on time; both belong to the *Oedipus at Colonus*. The first one is difficult, and certainly corrupt; yet it brings out the idea quite clearly. It begins in Aeschylean threat, saying: "Time sees all this, sees it always." [12] But then it goes on with a two-fold sentence, bringing in a distinction between different cases; and the end of the sentence says that time, in one day, raises one again. Whatever the exact text, which we shall not discuss here, it is sure that our former executor of justice is here supposed to act suddenly, with an unpredictable and arbitrary liberty belonging to its nature. Time has become the cause of all the ups and downs in life, which have no reason in themselves. This view recalls what Oedipus had said before, in a remark which is our second example: "To the gods alone comes never old age or death; all else is confounded by all-mastering time" (609: *pankratēs chronos*).

The same view about time recurs in all the plays; and even when it is not put forward quite so precisely, it is always borne out by the general trend of the play.

We have quoted, as a starting point, the song at the be-

[12] 1453: ὁρᾷ, ὁρᾷ ταῦτ' ἀεὶ χρόνος.

ginning of the *Trachinian Women;* but it could be added that, later in the play, the nurse remarks, to the same effect: "Rash is he who reckons on the morrow, or on days beyond it; for to-morrow is not, until to-day is safely past" (945–946). In *Ajax,* Athena makes it clear to Odysseus that man is but a fleeting shadow; everything in the tragedy suggests violent changes: Ajax, who was a proud warrior, now a poor madman; Tecmessa, who was of a rich family, now a slave; and everybody insists on this prevalence of change, with fiery emphasis. Not to mention, yet, the famous monologue of Ajax, there are Menelaus' words: "These things come by turns. This man was once hot and insolent; now 'tis my hour to be haughty" (1087–1088); and there are the chorus' remarks, at the conclusion: "Many things shall mortal learn by seeing; but, before he sees, no man may read the future or his fate" (1418–1420). Is that not what is repeated in the *Antigone,* with a clearer word and a new idea of fortune (*tuchē*)? For we read: "There is no state of mortal life that I would ever praise or blame as settled: fortune raises and fortune humbles the lucky or unlucky from day to day" (1156 ff.). Is it not what provides the main theme of the *Oedipus Rex?* Indeed, there we read, at the peripeteia, when Oedipus finds out the truth, a clear statement by the chorus: "Alas, generations of men, how mere a shadow do I count your life! Where, where is the mortal who wins more of happiness than just the seeming, and, after the semblance, a falling away?" (1186 ff.). This is the reason why the same play ends with the old maxim that no one should be called happy before his death.[13]

[13] Agamemnon mentions the idea in Aeschylus (*Aga.*, 928–929); it is put forward by Herodotus' Solon, not to mention other authors.

Now if we come to the *Philoctetes*, is it not obvious that the poor man provides an illustration of the same theme? Does he not speak himself of a succession of good and evil fortune? [14] Does he not add: "He who stands clear of trouble should beware of dangers; and when a man lives at ease, then it is that he should look most closely to his life, lest ruin should come on it by stealth"? Finally, the fate of Oedipus in the *Oedipus at Colonus* is but another example illustrating this major truth. It would be pointless to quote all the easy remarks about the reversal of his or other fortunes: they are too numerous, too much in agreement with the main trend of thought: it would be only insisting on the obvious.[15]

Indeed, this destructive action of time, which is clearly shown by the verbs describing it (such as *sunchein*, meaning "to confound," in *Oedipus at Colonus*, 609, or *marainein*, meaning "to extinguish," in *Ajax*, 713), is the very mark of human condition. Gods are not submitted to time.[16] This is what the chorus says in the *Antigone*, explaining that Zeus does not yield to sleep, or to the "untiring months of the gods: he remains on Olympus, ignorant of age." Similarly, the laws of the gods do not depend on time: they exist forever and have always ex-

[14] Cf. 503: *παθεῖν μὲν εὖ, παθεῖν δὲ θάτερα.*

[15] In *Oedipus at Colonus*, the main passages would be: 7 (about *αἱ πάθαι . . . χὠ χρόνος ξυνών*); 394 ("the gods lift thee now, but, before, they were working thy ruin"); 567–568 ("I know well that I am a man, and that in the morrow my portion is no greater than yours"); and 607–608 (quoted above, p. 93).

[16] In Aeschylus, the gods had a past and could change, as we see in the *Prometheus;* yet, we occasionally find the idea of all conditions being an alternate mixture of good and evil, except for the gods: see *Agamemnon*, 551 ff., with the conclusion: *τίς δὲ πλὴν θεῶν | ἅπαντ' ἀπήμων τὸν δι' αἰῶνος χρόνον.*

isted; they cannot be forgotten, for a divine power is in them, which "never grows old" (as we read in the *Oedipus Rex*).[17] Compared to them, man is a creature of one day, the child of the day; he is, according to a well-known formula, ephemeral: *hamerios anthrōpos.*[18]

We are reminded of Pindar—particularly the opposition between gods and men as regards time, which is so clearly stated at the end of the third Isthmian ode and in fragment 143.[19] And there we find also the ephemeral nature of man.[20] But it does not remind us only of Pindar: Herodotus also often insisted on the frailty of human things; some sentences of his are close to some of Sophocles' lines, even in the detail of words.[21] What is more, one may trace the thought to a philosopher like Heraclitus. For all this recalls Heraclitus' famous saying about time being "a child, playing with knuckle-bones—sovereignty

[17] For Zeus never growing old, see *Antigone* 609: ἀγήρως δὲ χρόνῳ. For the laws of the gods, the main texts are, of course, *Antigone*, 450 ff., and *Oedipus Rex*, 865 ff. The *Moirai* are μακραίωνες in *Antigone*, 987. Of the divine power, Sophocles says: οὐδὲ γηράσκει (*Oedipus Rex*, 871).

[18] *Ajax*, 399; *Antigone*, 790.

[19] Snell. See *Isthm.*, III, 18:

Αἰὼν δὲ κυλινδομέναις
ἁμέραις ἄλλ' ἄλλοτ' ἐξάλ-
λαξεν. ῎Ατρωτοί γε μὰν παῖδες θεῶν.

[20] See H. Fraenkel, "Man's Ephemeros Nature according to Pindar," *T.A.Ph.A.*, 1946, 131–145. The expression, it will be noted, does not occur in Aeschylus. For the unsteadiness in man's life, see *Ol.*, II, 33 ff., *Pyth.*, III, 107; IV, 291; XII, 28 ff. Before Pindar, one should, in fact, mention Archilochus: see fr. 7, Diehl, 1 Lasserre: ἄλλοτε δ' ἄλλος ἔχει τάδε· νῦν μὲν . . . ἐξαῦτις δ' ἑτέρους ἐπαμείψεται.

[21] Compare *Philoctetes*, 235: πολλὰ γὰρ τάδε ἐν τῶ μακρῷ γένοιτ' ἂν ἀνθρώπων χρόνῳ, and Herodotus, V, 9: γένοιτο δ' ἂν πᾶν ἐν τῷ μακρῷ χρόνῳ; or compare the use of κύκλος in Sophocles, as seen above, with Herodotus, I, 207: κύκλος τῶν ἀνθρωπηΐων ἐστὶ πρηγμάτων, περιφερόμενος δὲ οὐκ ἐᾷ αἰεὶ τοὺς αὐτοὺς εὐτυχέειν.

of a child" (whatever the exact meaning of some words).[22] In fact, many details in this alternate succession of contrary things remind us of Heraclitus and his linking them two by two in some sort of antithetic unity.[23] It has been suggested that, on the whole, Heraclitus' writings had not been without influence on Sophocles: the hypothesis has been supported, among others, by J. C. Kamerbeek, in a short article, where one can see that time and its oscillating changes provide the most convincing clue.[24] The question of influences is always rather difficult to settle, and we shall not take sides in the discussion. Yet, two points do emerge from it, and are of some interest to us: first, Sophocles' idea of time is coherent and strong enough to be compared with a philosopher's doctrine; but, secondly, this idea pervades so completely all his work, that, whether or not contemporary influences helped him in forming it, it is, in fact, his own; for it is deeply rooted in his whole view of life.

Sophocles' view stands to Heraclitus' philosophy in the same relation as did Aeschylus' to the old creed of pious times: it may have fed on this philosophy, but only because it was naturally in search of such food; and it finally brought out its own fruit, in a magnificent and free production.

One thought should be added. For Sophocles goes even further. In Opstelten's book about Sophocles' pessimism,

[22] Fr. 52: *Αἰὼν παῖς ἐστι παίζων, πεττεύων · παιδὸς ἡ βασιληΐη*. The meaning of *Αἰών* is doubted by Kirk.

[23] For other views common to both, see the article by Kamerbeek, mentioned in the following note. Among them, of course, is the famous saying: *ἦθος ἀνθρώπῳ δαίμων*.

[24] "Sophocle et Héraclite, quelques observations sur leurs rapports," in *Studia Vollgraff*, 1948, pp. 89–103.

we find lists of passages, some of which indicate transcience and instability or uncertainty, others insignificance, futility, and weakness of man and human existence.[25] In practically all of them time is directly or indirectly involved. And that is only natural, for time has an action not only on man's destiny but on his very feelings. In fact, the most important text about time, the one used by Kamerbeek to show the link with Heraclitus, is one that we have saved till now, for it clearly brings forward this new and important idea. It is the famous monologue by Ajax, by which his sailors are led to mistaken hope. If the song in the *Trachinian Women* dominated one group of texts, this one answers it in importance and in poetic power.

The monologue is partly deceptive, because Ajax says he has changed his mood to submission and has fully decided to live and obey, whereas in fact he has not changed, and will soon take his own life. But yet, what he says about the world at large agrees with Sophocles' general views about it; he only presses the idea somewhat further. For he emphasizes, as Sophocles so often does, the altering power of time, but extends the alteration to human feelings—which is something we had not seen before.[26] He begins: "All things the long and countless time first draws from darkness, then buries from light;[27] and there is nothing for which man may not look; the dread oath is

[25] Opstelten, *Sophocles and Greek Pessimism*, pp. 124 ff. He lists nine items, in a somewhat artificial distinction.

[26] On this distinction, see G. M. Kirkwood, *A Study of Sophoclean Drama* (Ithaca, 1958), pp. 160–162.

[27] 646 ff.: *Ἅπανθ' ὁ μακρὸς κἀναρίθμητος χρόνος | φύει τ' ἄδηλα καὶ φανέντα κρύπτεται*. The verbs used have a very general meaning. Yet, one might say there is, hidden behind them, an idea of the cycle of stars, as we have seen it above.

vanquished, and the stubborn will. For even I. . . ." Toward the end, making use of a classical saying of the wise Bias,[28] he brings into this ever-altering world even friendship and enmity: "For I am newly aware that our enemy is to be hated but as one who will hereafter be a friend; and toward a friend I would wish but thus far to show aid and service, as knowing that he will not always abide. For to most men the haven of friendship is false." It is true that Ajax, if sincerely aware of these things, is, to say the least, newly aware of them and thoroughly unhappy with them: his bitterness, therefore, exaggerates the ideas which he puts forward and which he cannot stop hating. But even though he should hate them, it is true that things do change. In fact Ajax' harsh emphasis is echoed by others, who take some milder steps in the same direction.

The main passage to be compared with Ajax' speech of deception is a speech by Oedipus, at the other end of Sophocles' career, in the *Oedipus at Colonus.* Here, the old Oedipus explains to Theseus how his city may later get into trouble with Thebes. Nothing suggests that he is wrong; and what he says is very near to what Ajax had said. "To the gods alone does old age or death never come: all else is confounded by all-mastering time (*pankratēs chronos;* 607 ff.). Earth's strength decays, and the strength of the body;[29] faith dies; distrust appears; and the same spirit is never steadfast among friends, or between city and city; for, be it soon or be it late, what was sweet becomes bitter, and then again is liked." Just as in the *Ajax,* one starts with the general condition of the universe and goes on to deal with human psychology and morals,

[28] Aristotle, *Rhetoric,* II, 1389b and 1395a—fragment 39.

[29] There is, in the Greek text, a repetition of the word φθίνει, which adds much power to the idea.

particularly with friendship. Of course the feeling is one of blame, or at least of regret. But Sophocles does not suggest that there is anything untrue in what Oedipus says. And the play was written when there was war with Thebes.

One may also add that, in the form of casual remarks, there are several other passages in Sophocles which express similar ideas.[30] The *Ajax,* which contains the main text, also contains the most numerous such references. For Ajax' soldiers, although filled with joy at the idea of his change, and admiring what he hates, describe the world's unsteadiness just as he does. "The strong years," they say, make all things fade; nor would I say that aught was too strange for belief, when thus, beyond our hopes, Ajax hath been led to repent of his wrath against the Atreidae, and his dread feuds" (713 ff.).

The translation quoted is Jebb's, and the text is also Jebb's. But it should be noticed that all the manuscripts have, at the end of the first sentence: ***marainei te kai phlegei,*** time "extinguishes and kindles," "puts out and brightens." So that we should have here the same alternate movement which, in its cosmic majesty, seems to have always haunted Sophocles' mind. Does it matter that these last words have no immediate application in the context? They have one in Sophocles' thought. And I feel quite convinced, with Kamerbeek, that they should be kept.[31]

[30] There is a well-known fragment, which has been often quoted, namely 868 N, 954 P: *χρόνος δ' ἀμαυροῖ πάντα κεἰς λήθην ἄγει*. But it is difficult to know in what mood and intention the remark was made.

[31] Mazon and Dain omitted them, as Jebb. Kamerbeek mentions the relation between *φλέγει* here and *φλέγειν* in 673, for the appearance of day, following night.

While criticizing Jebb, why not remark that his translation of *megas chronos* by "the strong years" is feeble and poor? In the three passages quoted till now, we have "the long and countless time," "all-mastering time," "the great time": how could one more strongly declare that the cause of the evil is one terrible power and one only—namely, the power of time? The least one should do is to keep the word, if not the richness of style.

To these passages, many others could be added where characters, whether with sadness or with revolt, utter similar remarks. "Ah! gratitude to the dead—in what quick manner it falls away from men . . . it is all forgotten, all flung aside" (this is Teucer, in *Ajax,* 1266 ff.). "Many people are friends at one time, who later on are foes" (this is Odysseus, in the same play, line 1359). "The human heart is inconstant to its joys" (this is Deianeira, in the *Trachinian Women,* 440). "Forget not your foes, but refrain from excess of wrath against them; for Time is a god who makes rough ways smooth" (this is the chorus in *Electra,* 179). This view of time is shared by too many characters in Sophocles' plays: it must, in some ways, express the poet's own doctrine. After all, his most personal song is probably the famous song about old age, in the *Oedipus at Colonus,* where we see that everything has flown away, leaving one without strength, or sociable mood, or friends.

But, if it is true that Sophocles' attention seems to have been more and more driven toward what regards man's feelings, this finally leaves us with a problem—an important one. For if man were such a puppet as these last passages suggest, there would be neither tragedy, nor greatness. There would not have existed a Sophocles.

✣ ✣

It may indeed have been noticed that many of the last views were uttered in the way of advice. One should be supple and not stubborn, patient and not fierce; one should submit to opportunity; one should submit to time. Now we come to the very core of Sophocles' moral problem: who says that? and is it true? and are there no other ways of dealing with time and of considering the relation between time and man? These questions must be considered, and they will perhaps take us a little farther into understanding the inner structure of Sophocles' plays.

We must certainly beware of refusing too soon the idea of obedience to time.

The advice which so many reasonable people give to the hero, would perhaps, if followed, hold him back from heroism. But even this does not mean that it is a low ideal, or one that was to be despised by the sociable and amicable man we know Sophocles to have been. When his characters use the idea in order to advise indulgence and forgiveness, who could pretend to see there a low ideal? That is the case, at least, with Odysseus, in the *Ajax*.[32] He refuses to laugh at Ajax in the beginning, for in that great downfall he sees a proof of human frailty; he understands that one day is enough to humble a man or raise him (as Athena says in line 132); therefore, he thinks a similar doom could befall him, and he feels but pity. His reaction is of the same kind near the end of the play. There he says, as Ajax had said before: "Many are friends at one

[32] Deianeira also speaks for tolerance.

time and then again are foes" (1359); yet the consequence he draws is not one of bitterness, but of tolerance and friendliness: "I am ready to be his friend—as staunch as I was a foe." In other words, it is quite possible to draw from that pessimistic view of life a rather noble philosophy of human solidarity. Man sees his own weakness, as he is a prey to time's arbitrary treatment; but he derives from that knowledge more prudence, more patience.

There is a way of accepting time, which amounts to a refusal to let time destroy more than is necessary in human society.

Had Sophocles only commended such an attitude, he would, even then, have been a noble writer and a worthy man—but not, perhaps, an author of great tragedies.

What produces the tragedy is the fact that, in some cases, some characters cannot yield. Either their nature forbids it, or the yielding would mean dishonor. More generally speaking, their nature forbids it because it means dishonor. It must be acknowledged that, except for the chorus and for Odysseus, who are not really tragic heroes, none of the characters who refer to this ideal of supple wisdom and patience does in fact follow it. Ajax, whether or not his words were really mendacious, certainly does not yield. Deianeira, like Ajax, says she does; but she plans a way to recover her husband, and, when it fails, she dies. Oedipus, at the end of his life, observes with regret the way in which people generally behave, but he does not, himself, behave after the same fashion: he never yields, never condones, never changes. The last play about him, the *Oedipus at Colonus,* may show his transfiguration into a god-protected and sacred hero: it does not show him as a saint or even as a humane person; till the very end, he acts in fierce and proud anger. It is therefore quite clear that, when Sophocles' real heroes mention the influence of time, their own final attitude is one of refusal. The characters who sincerely advocate the lessons of time are either unenlightened members of a chorus, as those who blame Antigone, or timid persons, whose advice only enhances the hero's or heroine's firmness, as Antigone's and Electra's more womanly sisters; [33] what is worse, they may also be stern tyrants, who seek in vain to be obeyed, as Creon does, both in the *Antigone* and in the *Oedipus at Colonus*, and as also do the two kings in command of the Greek fleet at Troy.[34]

Against such advice, the real heroes choose another way. They remain stubborn, that is to say firm and unchanged.

When there is a question of behavior, they choose to behave according to unchanging rules; that is what Antigone so proudly explains. She has disobeyed Creon's order, because it was but a fragile, ephemeral order: "And I did not suppose that decrees were of such force, that a mortal could override the unwritten and unfailing rules of heaven. For their life is not of to-day or yesterday, but from all time, and no man knows when they were first put forth" (453 ff.). The same heroes also choose to be approved, not now but after their death, and to win thereby immortal fame.[35] And they choose to be ap-

[33] See, particularly, *Electra*, 330 ff.: *κοὐδ' ἐν χρόνῳ μακρῷ διδαχθῆναι θέλεις | θυμῷ ματαίῳ μὴ χαρίζεσθαι κενά.*

[34] See, for instance, *Ajax*, 1077–1078: "Though a man's frame has grown mighty, he should look to fall, perchance, by a little blow."

[35] *Philoctetes*, 1419–1420, 1422.

proved not by living persons but by the dead, for such an approval will abide forever: "For I owe a longer allegiance to the dead than to the living: in that world I shall abide forever," says Antigone in the very beginning of the play (74–75). Finally, if necessary, these heroes choose death itself. Antigone accepts it, as better than yielding; Ajax kills himself, as better than living with an altered reputation and new mood. And so do Deianeira, Jocasta, and many others. Whatever the circumstances, Sophocles' heroes always refuse to change. In her long patience, Electra remains obstinate; she grows harder with time, but through passionate fidelity to herself.[36] As for Neoptolemus, his real problem is whether or not he may keep to unfaltering principles and to his true nature. He remarks once, "All is offence, when a man has forsaken his true nature, and is doing what does not befit him": [37] as the others do, he chooses to be himself, in spite of all.

This choice, which always amounts to a refusal of time's influence, and which often means death or the danger of death, is indeed what endows the action in Sophocles' plays with tragic quality, and controls the very structure of the dramas. Whether we think of Heracles in the *Trachinian Women,* of Ajax, of Antigone, of Electra, of Neoptolemus, or of the old Oedipus, whom Theseus welcomes in Colonus, we always find the

[36] Hence this triumph, on her part, when she finally scorns the alleged lessons of time (1464): "Time has taught me the prudence of agreeing with the stronger" (this answering and echoing Chrysothemis' advice, at 1013, where she thought the stronger were her mother and stepfather).

[37] *Philoctetes,* 902–903. About this idea of being true to oneself, see *Electra,* 1083–1085. Electra has no stronger wish than to keep her *κλέος* after death (985).

action centered around one character, whom events and individuals try to persuade or to break down; and, one after the other, he or she faces all threats and all dangers, even death when it comes to death—all in an ever-increasing solitude, which can mean despair, but never renunciation.

This tragic pattern, which it is so easy to detect in many of Sophocles' plays, is utterly different from what we found in Aeschylus; and it corresponds to a new tragic approach, equally centered on time. In Aeschylus, the tragic quality of the action at hand came from the fact that people were conscious of blindly obeying God's inescapable scheme for the achievement of justice. In Sophocles, it comes from the fact that they are conscious of boldly refusing to adapt themselves to the altering circumstances of life. In both cases, time is the great power. But in Aeschylus, it assumed a meaning as the instrument through which the gods realized their will; in Sophocles it creates a background against which it is for man to assert his own obstinacy. If time could ever be said to be conquered, it would be, in Aeschylus, by the power of the gods—in so far as they make the past remain alive, and join with the present and the future in one single reality—but it would be, in Sophocles, by sheer action of the hero's will, as he boldly places himself beyond the grip of time.

This is indeed a vigorous and positive view of what man can achieve. But it should be added that man's virtues are displayed in yet another way, where his relation to time is slightly different.

If, at the hour of danger and ruin, time can mean to the hero actual threat and challenge, it must be kept in mind that, in the long run, time may also confirm the value of what he has done.

Indeed, there is truth, in time. Time is where the real nature of things and people finally comes to light. We have seen, in the *Ajax*, time bringing things to light and hiding them again from our eyes. This meant that things existed, then existed no more. But there is another meaning of the expression "to bring to light." Light is what enables us to see and to judge. What has once happened remains under our eyes, for us to know. Still more safely, what has endured or has been repeated is, in a way, confirmed by time—particularly so in human behavior. Is one a coward or not, a true friend or not? The answers are generally known with experience. We learn them in the long run; we learn them with time, *chronō(i)*. Conversely, if, for a while, something can be doubted or a lie avail, how is truth to be restored if not in some way or other through the help of time?

In this case, time is not a master whose wishes we may obey or refuse: it is but a witness, who knows everything and never retires. While leaving us the perfect right of acting as we want to, it has the power of proving, in the end, whether we acted as we should have done.

This idea is—once more—a common one in Greece, as early as the sixth century. Thales already spoke about time "finding out" everything (*aneuriskein*, as we saw p. 51). Later on, we find Solon counting on time to show that he was not mad, and emphatically repeating that time "will show" (*deixei*).[38] As for Theognis, he states that liars will be known in time: "Time brings to full

[38] Fr. 8 Hiller:

δείξει δὴ μανίην μὲν ἐμὴν βαιὸς χρόνος ἀστοῖς,
δείξει ἀληθείης ἐς μέσον ἐρχομένης.

light the true nature of each" (967: *ekphainei*). When we come to the fifth century, we again find Pindar, who has the most striking formulas of all, when he speaks about time "who alone establishes the correct truth" or about the days to come, which are the wisest witness.[39] It should be noted that Aeschylus himself occasionally presents us with the idea.[40] After Sophocles, it is very freely used by Euripides[41] and soon becomes a proverbial saying.[42]

But in Sophocles it has a great and characteristic importance. For it not only appears in numerous fragments, as that "no lie abides with time," or that "time uncovers all things and brings them to light," or that "time, seeing all and hearing all, unfolds all things";[43] it is also a main feature in the structure of one of Sophocles' most famous tragedies, the *Oedipus Rex.* There, the idea is repeatedly put forward, by various characters. Among the main passages, there is one where Creon advises Oedipus not to form any rash or hasty judgments, and

[39] *Olympian*, X, 53–55: ὅ τ' ἐξελέγχων μόνος | ἀλάθειαν ἐτήτυμον | χρόνος. On it goes with κατέφρασεν: time explains what has taken place—*Ol.*, I, 33–34: ἁμέραι δ' ἐπίλοιποι μάρτυρες σοφώτατοι. See also fr. 159 (40 Puech) about time being the best savior of worthy men.

[40] It comes in about small details; for instance, in the *Suppliants*, 993, about getting to know other people (their society ἐλέγχεται χρόνῳ), or in the *Agamemnon*, about getting to know the lion (727: χρονισθεὶς δ' ἀπέδειξεν ἦθος τὸ πρὸς τοκέων). The confidence in time, for bringing glory to the author, is linked with this idea; yet, it is slightly different, for it implies not only truth, but justice (similarly, Bacchylides, 13, 204–207): see below, p. 110.

[41] See below, p. 117.

[42] See Xenophon, *Hellenica*, III, 3, 2: συνεμαρτύρησε δὲ ταῦτ' αὐτῷ καὶ ὁ ἀληθέστατος λεγόμενος χρόνος εἶναι.

[43] These are fragments 59 N, 62 P; 832 N, 918 P; 280 N, 301 P. In the last two, the verbs are ἐκκαλύπτειν, εἰς φῶς ἄγειν, ἀναπτύσσειν.

reminds him that this is particularly important when one has to judge a virtuous man: "Nay, you will learn these things with sureness in time, for time alone shows a just man (*deiknusin*); whereas you could discern a knave even in one day" (613–615). But the idea is of course more striking when it applies to the hero himself; and from that point of view what indeed could be more striking than what the chorus says, when all is known at last, and the Theban elders exclaim, in the beginning of the last strophe of their song: "Time the all-seeing has found you out in your despite." [44]

This finding out, through the action of time, has been the very subject matter of the whole tragedy. It begins in ignorance, in error, in mistaken condemnations. As the play develops, the inquest goes on, exploring the past, which indeed is progressively "brought to light," "unfolded," "uncovered," so that, in a way, we have something which might remind us of the structure in the *Agamemnon*. In the *Agamemnon*, however, the facts themselves were known and only the connection was being looked for, in trembling and anguish. Here, the connection is put forward by official decision: the murderer, when known, will be destroyed; and the simple knowledge of his father's name will immediately ruin the hero. But this name is not known. Who was Laius' murderer? Who was Oedipus' victim? Who were Oedipus' parents? All the answers will be found—in time, leaving the hero to be destroyed by his discovery: "Time the all-seeing has found you out in your despite." It could be added that were these facts somewhat deceptive, time would correct

[44] 1213: ἐφηῦρε.

the impression they could make upon us; for it seems characteristic enough that Sophocles should have felt the need of presenting, in a later play, the death and ultimate glory of his hero.

This idea that time finds out the truth is not very different from Aeschylus' own confidence in time, when he trusted it would show the merits of his tragedies; and it brings us back to some sort of justice, not unlike our starting point. But the shift of emphasis in the structure of the plays or the comments made by the characters leaves no possible doubt about the difference in doctrine. If in both authors we find much that is similar—and in the first instance a similar insistance on time, as implying man's doom and uncertainty—the light in which Sophocles sees time is wholly different. Whether one accepts it in order to build on such foundations a sociable humanism, or refuses it in a fierce assertion of self, or counts on it to be a witness to human virtues, time, in Sophocles, only provides the background against which man's own action and person stand out, in his doomed greatness.

As we have examined Sophocles' ideas about time, we have been progressively led into examining with him man's moral problems. But before we leave him, we must still notice one last consequence of the shift in emphasis that has just been described.

As Sophocles considers time from the point of view of man, admitting quick changes of circumstances, which affect his fortunes and feelings, it follows in a natural way that the reckoning of time, and the length of it, are also considered, in his plays, from the same angle. His characters live in anxious waiting, as did Aeschylus' characters—and perhaps even more so, as urgency is now one of the main features of this theater. But they do not wait for generations. Their standard is not the family's life; it is their own happiness or misery. Time is therefore an internal and psychological experience.

This could bring us to a long discussion: let me quote only one small detail. There is much stress laid in *Ajax* on the "long retirement" of Ajax, which, in fact, may have lasted a few days, and much stress laid on his "long and difficult" recovery, which, in fact, may have lasted a few hours.[45] Length of time has indeed become more subjective; and Bruno Snell could well find in this evolution a new proof of his theories about what he called, in the title of his book, "the discovery of the mind." Time has now entered man's soul.

There we shall find it settled, well within, in the most subjective of our three poets—I mean, of course, Euripides.

[45] 193: *μακραίωνι . . . σχολᾷ*; 306: *μόλις πως . . . ξὺν χρόνῳ*.

5 *Time in Euripides*

When asked about a question of grammar raised by a sentence in Plato, my former master Paul Mazon used to say, in a tone of thorough scepticism: "One can find anything in Plato." The same would apply with more accuracy to Euripides—not to his grammar, but to his art and doctrines. Yet, even though he has tried so many paths, and given word to so many discordant voices, there is in his theater a quality of personal emotion, which rings in every single line and is easily known as his own. This twofold character, joining versatility and inner originality, can be traced in his view of time, and will provide us with a leading thread, which we shall follow, starting with what is less personal before we reach the core of his sensibility to the experience of time.

✣

Some of Euripides' remarks, some of his scenes, or even of his plays, seem to reproduce the Aeschylean tradition. Yet, even in those, it is easy to see that the inner spirit has faded away, and there appears a decline toward everyday life and common experience.

The play that is by far the most Aeschylean in its theme and spiritual trend is one that was written at the very end of Euripides' life. The history of the arts knows such paradoxical examples: archaism is a tentative coquettishness for innovators, after they have tried many a new fashion. In the *Bacchae*, we see a god inflicting misery as a punishment of ancient offence, committed a generation ago.[1] And the chorus, which is composed of faithful followers of Dionysus, highly advocates the old creed of time bringing out justice—with formulas which could belong to Aeschylus. One of them is very characteristic; it comes at line 882 and following: "The power of the gods acts in a slow but sure manner: they correct those among mortals who, in their mad fantasy, exalt their unbelief and do not respect things divine. While the foot of time treads on, they have many a subtle way to keep it hidden from unholy men, as they track them along." All is there: god, justice, delays, and time (in fact, even the famous "foot of time" which caused the scandal we have seen).[2] All—except, perhaps, the approval of the poet, who certainly does not try, in his play, to convey the idea that Dionysus acts according to real justice.

Such comments are not rare, even in other plays, but they are equally artificial and independent of the general trend of the play. In the *Heracles* (777 ff.), we read in a chorus-song that the man who has broken the law cannot

[1] The fact that it is a personal offense, not a sin against justice, is, of course, a sign of Euripides' difference from Aeschylus. God's justice, with him, is highly unjust.

[2] See above, p. 57.

face the future (exactly: "the coming back of time"), for the chariot of his prosperity will tumble to pieces.[3] Aeschylus might have said the same, with the image of a vessel; but where do we see that happening in the play? Perhaps in the tyrant's doom, which does not count as much as Heracles' own madness. In the *Ion*, Athena says "It is true that, always, what comes from the gods does require time, but proves in the end to be not lacking power";[4] but where does justice appear in the play? No wrong action is punished; no good one has its reward. And the person who claims divine action is, in fact, a goddess.

This discrepancy is to be kept in mind, when we are confronted with all the orthodox utterances, kept for us in the fragments: ancient scholars were highly moral people, and they were, no doubt, quite happy to pick up such commendable thoughts. Hence their number. In some of them, the speaker merely advises people not to acquire profit through unjust behavior, as it would not abide (as in the *Erechtheus*, fr. 362, 12). Others express a mere wish not to arouse god's wrath, for it is powerful, even when long delayed (as in the *Philoctetes*, fr. 800). Some more frankly conform to Aeschylean orthodoxy, as the one from the *Antiope* (fr. 223): "Justice, indeed, justice can come late (*chronios*) yet it falls from above before having been noticed, once it gets hold of an

[3] The image of the chariot race is already present in the "coming back of time": χρόνου τὸ πάλιν.

[4] 1614–1615:

> . . . ἀεὶ γὰρ οὖν
> χρόνια μὲν τὰ τῶν θεῶν πως, ἐς τέλος δ'οὐκ ἀσθενῆ.

The Budé translation says "la justice divine," thus indicating the underlying trend of thought.

impious man"; this could have been Aeschylus' speaking. The same can be said of fragment 510 (of unknown authorship): "It is impossible to escape unnoticed when one does what is wrong, for Time has a sharp eye and he sees everything." [5] These remarks, and others, that could be added easily,[6] do not lead us very far. And they remain isolated. Indeed, it all looks as if what formerly was a strongly felt doctrine, underlying whole plays, had now faded out and weakened into a sort of conventional stock.

In a similar way, the theme about the lessons of time often recurs in Euripides; but then either it is confined to suspect and low characters, as the nurse in the *Hippolytus* or the herald in the *Suppliants*, who pretend to act according to some pessimistic experience of life,[7] or it is linked with the idea of the versatility of time, not of the justice time produces. This new link is what appears from the fact that this lesson is qualified with the very un-Aeschylean word *poikilōtaton*, that is to say, "most diverse and variegated." [8]

This evolution reminds us of what we have seen of the progression from Aeschylus to Sophocles. We also find in Euripides some very Sophoclean affirmations.

[5] The Greek reads:

οὐκ ἔστι πράσσοντάς τι μοχθηρὸν λαθεῖν,
ὀξὺ βλέπει γὰρ ὁ χρόνος, ὃς τὰ πάνθ' ὁρᾷ.

[6] One could quote *Rhesus*, 893, very affirmative, but as an isolated formula, in a suspected play.

[7] See *Hippolytus*, 252: πολλὰ διδάσκει μ' ὁ πολὺς βίοτος; but she goes on saying that one shouldn't have too much affection for others; also *Suppliants*, 419: ὁ γὰρ χρόνος μάθησιν ἀντὶ τοῦ τάχους | κρείσσω δίδωσιν; but this means one should leave politics to the aristocrats. In *Peleus* (fr. 619), the lesson of time is brought back to ἐμπειρία and leads to simple prudence (cf. ἀσφαλέστερον).

[8] *Bellerophon*, fr. 291, 3: ὁ γὰρ χρόνος δίδαγμα ποικιλώτατον.

To begin with the more positive side of Sophocles' doctrine, we naturally find in Euripides that time discloses what man is worth and is a witness to his good or bad qualities.[9] In the same passage where the chorus of the *Heracles* exalts the god's just intervention, it emphasizes the influence of time, as having revealed the true worth of Heracles (805: *edeixe*). In the same scene of the *Hippolytus* where the nurse bitterly mentions the lessons of time, Phaedra finds an elaborate and slightly far-fetched image to show the revealing power of time: "As for the evil-doers among mortals, time reveals them, when the chance comes, by showing them a mirror, as to a young girl."[10] But it must be noticed that such remarks are not only marred by inappropriate wording: they have in a majority of cases debased the idea and brought it down to a sort of detective level. Truth will out. But truth no longer means the inner quality of man: truth is a matter of plain facts. Such is the case in the *Hippolytus*, when Hippolytus complains that Theseus will not wait till time enlightens him: he will not admit "time's evidence" (1051); and later Artemis also reproaches him with not having consulted time and reflection.[11] We find similar ideas in numerous fragments.[12] In two of them, we have the verb *deiknusi* (time "shows");[13] in one of

[9] There is also one short allusion to divine time and principles of old (*Bacchae*, 895–896: *τό τ'ἐν χρόνῳ μακρῷ | νόμιμον ἀεὶ φύσει τε πεφυκός*). But they are principles of old, not eternal ones. And, generally, Euripides prefers to insist on principles valid "for all Greeks" rather than "in all times"!

[10] 430. The verb is *ἐξέφηνε*. About this image, see above, p. 51.

[11] 1322: *οὐ χρόνῳ μακρῷ σκέψιν παρέσχες.*

[12] See, particularly, fragments 60 (*Alexander*); 112 (*Alope*); 733, 8 (*Phaëthon*); the second one is where the talkative habits are mentioned; in the last one, the text deals with a question of fact.

[13] 222 (*Antiope*); 303, 4 (*Bellerophon*).

them *alētheuein* (it "provides truth").[14] Several have quite elaborate images, speaking not only of time's decisive evidence (fr. 60: *tekmēriō(i)*), but about time's exact measurements (fr. 303, 4: *kanonas*), or about time's revelations and talkative habits: this refined imagery has been studied in another chapter.[15] But it may well be doubted if the real bearing of these suggestions was much wider than it is in the preserved plays; and it may be assumed that in most cases it was a mere matter of finding out the real facts, in plays where elaborate intrigues often rested on their being ignored or dissimulated by crafty lies. Just as Aeschylus' faith in the gods' justice has decayed when transported into Sophocles plays, just so has Sophocles faith in man's value declined and faded away, when transported into Euripides. What has survived has lost its acuteness.

But among Sophocles' ideas about time, one could easily be transplanted into Euripides without losing anything.[16] Once deprived of its optimistic complement, the idea of the unsteadiness of life, as the result of time, was a perfect theme for Euripides' pessimism. He takes up what Sophocles said of the short time sufficient for great change. But he insists that "*one single day*" is quite enough: "*one single day*" has deprived Hecuba of all her prosperity (*Hecuba*, 285). "*One single day*" has ruined the glorious fate of Amphitryon (*Heracles*, 510); indeed

[14] 441 (*Hippolytus*).

[15] See above, pp. 51–52.

[16] Some themes may of course have started in Euripides and been borrowed by Sophocles. We are trying to establish not an actual chronology but a general and logical relation.

the poet adds an image: chance has brushed it off, as a feather in the air. On the whole, "*one single day*" can upset and raise (fr. 420, 2).[17] Who knows what will happen in the course of the day? This question is asked by the chorus, speaking to Phaedra, in the *Hippolytus*, line 369; and after her death Hippolytus exclaims in awe that he has just left her (907), and "it was not long ago" that she still was looking on the light of day.

Indeed, anything can happen, at any time. There is a well-known group of verses repeated at the end of several tragedies, saying that many things occur that were unforeseen, and nothing happens as one thought it would.[18] This very unexpectedness of events, which is exactly the reverse of Aeschylus' doctrine, and goes further than most of Sophocles' statements, is often introduced in connection with time—more precisely with the human experience of time, man's life, man's *aiōn*. Anything can come from this *aiōn*.[19] It is fickle: "ever shifting to and fro" (*Hippolytus*, 1109), and "devoid of any steadiness" (*Orestes*, 980).[20] What is more, its changes occur by chance, and always with a destroying and sad influence.

The great similes in Sophocles could be reconciled with the idea of a possible order escaping man's understanding: with Euripides, time is the realm of *tuchē*, or "chance." In the *Hippolytus*, when the hero has just left, after having been cursed by his father, the women of the

[17] We have, in the different passages: ἦμαρ ἓν—ἡμέρᾳ μιᾷ—μί' ἡμέρα.

[18] See *Alcestis*, 1159 ff., among others.

[19] See *Heraclidae*, 898–900; this is the passage where Αἰών is χρόνου (or Κρόνου: see above, p. 37) παῖς.

[20] The words are πολυπλάνητος and ἀστάθμητος.

chorus say that they begin to doubt providence when they behold men's fortunes and their deeds (*tuchais*): "for one change follows upon another, coming from one direction or other; and life (*aiōn*) is perpetually transformed, shifting to and fro." We find the same idea in a number of passages.[21] Two of them are worth quoting: they offer the particular interest that they could easily be developed in Aeschylean terms, and yet insist on both hazard and misery. One is in the *Orestes*, where the chorus sings about the doomed family: "Alas! Miserable tribes of men, creatures of one day, living amid tears, behold how unpredictable are the ways of destiny. Various men know various sorrows, each in his turn, in the long course of time, and in the whole life of mortals nothing ever abides." [22]

But already in the *Heracles*, Amphitryon was complaining: "See my case: I was admired among mortals for my fame; but chance took it all away (ἡ τύχη), as a feather lifted up in the air—in one single day." [23]

Amphitryon's great fame did not abide. Nothing does. This change is not a special challenge, nor this misery part of a heroic destiny. Sooner or later, men, in Euripides, are deprived of what they enjoyed.[24]

[21] Including fr. 304, 4 (from *Bellerophon*):

τὸ μὲν μέγ' εἰς οὐδὲν ὁ πολὺς χρόνος
μεθίστησι, τὸ δὲ μεῖον αὔξων (or, with Musgrave: αὔξει).

[22] 976 ff. One will notice the two series of words: πολύπονα—πήματα, on one hand; παρ'ἐλπίδας, ἀμείβεται, ἀστάθμητος, on the other.

[23] 506 ff. The idea of appreciating each day that passes without pain is more pessimistic than the advice of enjoying it, as we find it in Aeschylus, *Persians*, 840, and in Euripides, *Suppliants*, 953.

[24] See fr. 273, 2 (from *Auge*), ending with the sad conclusion: κοὐδεὶς διὰ τέλους εὐδαιμονεῖ.

Sometimes, it is true, Euripides makes a virtuous effort to suggest that only ill-acquired prosperity is fragile, or that only external goods are easily lost. Thus it happens that, in the *Electra* (938 ff.), the good nature is said to remain unaltered; and this could sound as a sort of pre-stoicism and consolation. But the remark is caught between two developments about the unsteadiness of things, and seems only to give them, by contrast, greater emphasis.[25] In fact, this quality of the soul is no great consolation! it does not help. What is the advantage of virtue? asks a desolate chorus in the *Heracles* (669 ff.): gods make no difference and "life in its revolving movement favors nothing but wealth." But another character, in the *Aeolus*, said in even worse bitterness that even nobility in man amounted to nothing but wealth, and came and went with it: "It comes in cycle; one gets it, the other has it not" and "whoever keeps it longer is a noble man" (fr. 22, 5).

This impression of unsteadiness is therefore the same as in Sophocles—yet not the same. It has not only lost the positive complement which heroism and fame provided in Sophocles: its very majesty has changed into a tiring and dispiriting disorder, where the changes are more perpetual, more unforeseen, more absurd.

This should not surprise us. If the shift from Aeschylus to Sophocles could be explained by the fact that time had first been considered from the point of view of the gods,

[25] 938–944. First, it is said that wealth disappears, *σμικρὸν ἀνθήσας χρόνον*, then, that wealth without justice lasts but *βράχυν . . . χρόνον*. The idea that moral qualities always remain the same is only mentioned here for the sake of contrast, between two statements insisting on unsteadiness.

and then in its effect on man and as part of a dialogue where man was to answer, then we can admit that the same evolution goes on with Euripides. Time now is seen but from the point of view of man's sensibility. Hence comes this impossibility of mentioning its unsteadiness without adding, as we did, that it is a tiring and dispiriting disorder. Time is judged from the standards of our suffering. Time is mixed up in our emotions.

These emotions are more varied and personal. They follow the rhythm of time and conform to its bright or sombre hues, whether for the future or the past. But the main difference is that, whether for the future or the past, these emotions are not only stirred by the main action and its general trend: they follow all the small movements of everyday life; and the length of time which the characters consider seems long only by the subjective standards of impatience and fear, or relief and regret.

As regards impatience and fear, this new perspective might easily suggest a sort of decline. These feelings had been very powerfully described by Aeschylus, and very dramatically presented by Sophocles: when we come to Euripides, they are to be found everywhere, but often with a shorter range—as if we were confronted with many small, hurried waves, instead of one long continuous gale. In Aeschylus the emotions were great according to the importance of what they applied to: in Euripides, what they apply to seems great according to their own standards, which are personal and sentimental

—and what is said about time is only a sign of the quality of the emotion.

"The time is long, already, since. . . ." This beginning could suit the majesty of one of Aeschylus' long reflections on the past, or the pathetic longing of Sophocles' heroes.[26] But in the *Heracles* it expresses only the tyrant's impatience for the time his victims take in preparing themselves (702: "The time is long, already, since you began dressing yourselves with the robes and garments of the dead"). The time, of course, was short; the statement only shows Lycus' cruel impatience and conveys thereby an impression of urgency. This impatience is by no means weaker in the victims when they hope for release. Megara knows there may be hope in waiting, but she suffers and complains: "Time, in the interval, hurts me and bites me," she says.[27]

And, very often, Euripides stops to describe that impatience, which starts and stirs the action.

He does it for the normal restlessness of the soldiers in Aulis (a restlessness that is, indirectly, a cause of the whole series of events): he imagines and quotes their words, in a lively, human complaint: "Achilles, what are we waiting for? What kind of time must we still count and measure out, till we start for Troy?" (815). He does it also in more serious cases, where he seems to take an artistic pleasure in describing this very impatience of

[26] The expression here (*χρόνος γὰρ ἤδη δαρός*) can be compared with the words of Ajax (*Ajax*, 414):

πολὺν πολύν με δαρόν τε δὴ
κατείχετ' ἀμφὶ Τροίαν χρόνον

[27] *Ibid.*, 94: *ὁ δ' ἐν μέσῳ με λυπρὸς ὢν δάκνει χρόνος.*

desire, when desire will lead to disaster. "Take me there quickly! I grudge the delay," exclaims Pentheus in the *Bacchae* (820): he is urging Dionysus to take him to the mountain, where he will meet his death.

But then, any delay is too long for real emotion. And impatience can often feed on a short length of time. Therefore we can find in the tragedies numerous passages that express longing or fear, both with impatience, yet with no special mention of time; and, on the other hand, the mention of time does not imply any really long time, but only the rhythm of life, brimming with its natural urgency. Time is what we make it to be. To revert to the *Iphigeneia*, we can remember how Clytemnestra comes out, waiting for her husband: he has been away a short time, but, as all the future rests on what he will say or do, she is restless with impatience and cannot wait within: "He has been away long," she says (1099: *chronion*).

All these people who "have been away long" in Euripides, raising either impatience or concern, explain one's coming out or getting in, or entering such and such a course of actions. "Am I late? Have you been worrying?" asks Xuthus of his wife in the *Ion* (403). "What shall I say if I am long away?" asks the servant in the *Andromache* (84). "He has been gone long, and is not to be seen," says Hector in the *Rhesus* (559). From the great passions to the small devices regarding practical arrangement of events this sentimental consideration of time is always of the same nature.[28] It shows how each man

[28] This even helps in practical devices: see *Ion*, 1130, where the father explains what to do in case he should be late (μακρὸν χρόνον μένω). This petty precision takes us very far indeed from Aeschylus.

depends on the others, and has to adjust his feelings to the others' behavior.

At the same time, it shows that real time is nothing in itself: what makes it long or short is one's desires and fears. An ill man will be impatient to walk: "He has not walked for so long" (*Orestes*, 234: *chronion*); a sleepless woman will find the night long and say, with Phaedra, "in the long time of night." [29]

This emotional quality of time appears even more clearly when the past and the present are brought in contrast. In Euripides' psychology of emotion the past has a great importance in its relation to present moods, whether sad or happy.

This tendency shows in his picture of relief. Long passages of his are but sentimental commentaries on the simple idea, "at last!"

Sometimes it is but simple relief at the idea that justice has come: so in the *Heracles*, when Alcmena exclaims that "at last" Zeus has pitied her (869: *chronō(i)*) and "at last" her foe is in her hand (941: *chronō(i)*).

But in many scenes where parents come together after a long separation, this "at last" spreads into exclamations, and comments, and long, passionate remembrances of former impatience. In the *Electra*, we find such a scene when Orestes and Electra are brought together: "At last, you are here, with me, unexpectedly," exclaims Electra (578: *chronō(i)*); and Orestes answers: "And you with me, at last" (579: *chronō(i)*); they go on re-

[29] *Hippolytus*, 375: νυκτὸς ἐν μακρῷ χρόνῳ. We do not mention here lines where χρόνῳ just means "after a while," as in the speech by the messenger in *Hippolytus*, 1181. For the evolution, see above, p. 44.

membering how they doubted, before, that such joy would befall them; and the chorus joins in: "You did come, O long-desired day" (585: *chronios*); and again later, when they have succeeded, Electra says that Aegisthus has been found out, "at last" (952: *chronō(i)*); the joy of this sentimental relief indeed inspires the one little regret at the end of the play: Orestes must leave his sister, whom he had found "at last" (*chronian*).

When a husband and wife come together in the *Helen*, their emotion is even more strongly emphasized. Helen finds her husband "at last" (566: *chronios*), but there remains some difficulty before they can be sure of what has taken place. When they are, there is a whole scene of joy and relief: "O much desired day!" exclaims Menelaus; and Helen: "The time has been long indeed, but just now joy has come." [30] And on they go, yielding to tender emotions, and mentioning this "husband who came at last" (645: *chronion*). This way of remembering past impatience in order to enhance present joy is quite characteristic of Euripides. In the same play, it will recur when the king believes he will "at last" have Helen for a wife (1232: *chronia*), or when the chorus sings about Helen's returning to Greece, "at last" (1468: *chronō(i)*).

In the *Phoenician Women*, the return of Polynices does not give rise to fewer at last's. "At last," says Antigone, his sister, in her wish to embrace him (166: *chronō(i)*); "at last" says the chorus (295: "you came, oh, with time!"); "at last," exclaims his mother: "At last I see your face, after thousands of days"; [31] whereas Polynices himself weeps for emotion when he sees the

[30] 625: ὁ μεν χρόνος | παλαιός.

[31] 305: χρόνῳ σὸν ὄμμα μυρίαις τ'ἐν ἁμέραις | προσεῖδον.

palace at last (367: *chronios*). Then follows a whole scene of questions and remembrances about the time when he was away.[32]

The examples are too numerous for me to mention them all.[33] There is in all the plays of Euripides a perpetual state of emotion, which often causes the characters to turn their attention to themselves, and also to turn it toward the past—even to the point of indulging in self-pity, as does Creüsa in the *Ion,* when she sees the piece of material she had embroidered many years ago: "O ancient work of my maiden toil!" (1425: *chronion*).

This tendency is well illustrated by the use the author makes of the adjective *chronios.* This adjective is used twice by Aeschylus, four times by Sophocles, and twenty-nine times by Euripides. He likes to transfer the affective quality of people's feelings to the person or event affecting them: their emotions pervade all reality and have become the only standards to describe the world.[34]

It should be added that this strong habit of emotional self-pity is of course more easily found when the charac-

[32] See also, later, 1043: *χρόνῳ δ' ἔβα.*

[33] See, for instance, *Iphigeneia in Tauris,* 258 (*χρόνιοι γὰρ ἥκουσ'*); *Orestes,* 475 (*χρόνιος εἰσιδὼν φίλον*) and 485; also *Iphigeneia in Aulis,* which is fairly rich—419, of Orestes, brought at last to his father (*χρόνον παλαιὸν δωμάτων ἔκδημος ὤν*); 636, of Iphigeneia, wishing to kiss her father after so long (*διὰ χρόνου*); or 640, rejoicing that she sees him at last (*πολλῷ χρόνῳ*); or 660, regretting his long absence (*πολὺν ἀπῆσθα χρόνον*).

[34] Of course, the affective coloration may be more or less important. It is practically absent in *Electra,* 1157. It will be noticed that the adjective may also mean "long-continued," "lasting": this is, characteristically enough, the most frequent meaning in Pindar (see *Pyth.,* III, 115; *Nem.,* IV, 6; *Ol.,* IV, 9).

ters meet not with joy but with sorrow. In that case, the tendency which causes them to turn to their own pain and dwell on their own past produces a sort of lament about things that are no more. This is particularly Euripidean. Andromache thus broods over the past of Troy and over her own: she "inspired envy, on former days, Andromache, but now. . . .[35] Hecuba also meditates sadly on a similar contrast; she is a fellow slave to the Trojan women "yet, formerly their queen" (61) and later again she says: "I was a queen before, and now your slave; I was happy in my children, and now an old woman and one without children" (809–810). The same reflection can bring out heroic deeds: it does with Polyxena, who declares proudly that her father was a king of all Phrygia, that she was brought up to marry a prince, was to be wooed and to command and be looked at by all, almost as a goddess; "and now I am a slave" (357): hence, her resolution to die. This deep contrast between past and present is a key to many pathetic utterances in Euripides: when Hecuba remembers all the sweet habits of the child Astyanax, in the *Trojan Women*, it gives to her sorrow a terribly cruel acuteness: how his mother used to arrange his hair; how Hecuba enjoyed seeing the likeness to his father; how he used to boast, and promise things; how she herself used to caress him and look at him asleep: all that "is gone" (1188). And when the poet wants to convey the horror of Troy's sudden capture, instead of describing directly this horror, as Aeschylus would have done, he

[35] *Andromache*, 5; all the words, and their emphatic position, add to the pathetic nature of the contrast:

> ζηλωτὸς ἔν γε τῷ πρὶν Ἀνδρομάχη χρόνῳ,
> νῦν δ'. . . .

describes in contrast the happy memory of peace just before: in the *Hecuba*, the women sing of the time of night when they were preparing their hair, while their husbands were resting close by; in the *Trojan Women*, they sing of feast and dance; then comes the shouting and murdering. And all that was is gone.[36]

This habit of perpetually contrasting the past and present times adds to the pathos. For, being a good psychologist, Euripides knows that joy and misery are complementary emotions, which show one against the other. Indeed he occasionally reminds us of the traditional observation according to which misery is worse when succeeding happiness. This was neither new nor original;[37] and Thucydides says the same in the Funeral Oration;[38] but it may be characteristic that Euripides chose to emphasize it, and went so far as to say that it is better to be always unhappy.[39] However, he also chose to enhance the emotions of his characters by such contrasting conditions, and to comment on their feelings. In the *Heraclidae*, Iolaus says he and the children are like sailors in a rough sea: they thought they were touching land and were safe, and then (*eita*) they are brushed away to the high seas again (*palin*); and he complains: "Alas, why did you

[36] The chorus uses the word φροῦδος in bitter irony, telling Zeus he won't get any more sacrifices (1071 ff.: φροῦδαί σοι θυσίαι . . .).

[37] Pindar (*Pyth.*, IV, 291) already introduces the idea with φαντί: "they say that . . ." That this is an ever discussed topic shows in Musset's lines, in *Souvenir:* "Dante, pourquoi dis-tu qu'il n'est pire misère/Qu'un souvenir heureux dans les jours de douleur . . . ?" (which is almost a direct quotation from *Inferno* Canto V, 119–120, which is a quotation, in its turn, from Boethius).

[38] II. 44. 2.

[39] *Iph. Taur.*, 1117–1122; cf. fr. 285, 15–20.

cheer me up a moment ago, O wretched hope, when your favor was not to be continued?" (433–434).

Past hope makes disappointment more bitter; past fear makes relief sweeter. As all Euripides' theater is centered on pathos, no doubt this explains two main features in the structure of his tragedies.

First it explains why he relies so much on what we call "coup de théâtre," meaning an unexpected event which arrives at the very last minute, when the agony has been so long kept up that all hope was gone. At this very minute, at last, there comes the savior, or the right explanation about who is who; pathos is thus at its highest.

The same reason also explains why his tragedies are built on so many various incidents and sudden changes, on *peripeteiai*. Indeed Iolaus and Heracles' children were without hope; then they are saved, then rejected again, then saved again. Our sympathy undergoes the same stimulating changes of emotion that the person we see experiences and describes. And as the action in the late plays of Euripides grows more and more complex, this result is also better achieved. Where Aeschylus counted on continuity, and Sophocles on one clear fight and reaction, Euripides has to use the alternate movement of contrasting events. Each author's view of time controls the structure of his plays.

Euripides' view of time thus appears as a psychological one. It centers on emotion. It shows in emotion. For all our personal life, marked by hope and regret, by fear and relief, is entwined with the idea of time. The experience of time is itself of an emotional nature. It is easy enough to see how much psychology gained by such shift of attention. All of a sudden, one could say, modern psychology has come to life, with all its subtleties and richness.

That this progress rests on a philosophical renunciation is only logical: what has been lost for theological consideration or even for cosmical meditation has been gained for the study of man himself, in his painful passions and toil. Psychology is linked with religious pessimism.

It might well be wondered if, to Euripides at least, psychology offered no remedy and no compensation—in other words, if his plays never suggest any way of escaping the perpetual oscillations of time and misery. Is there, for him, no way out?

By a beautiful paradox, it seems that time may in some cases become a healer—and precisely because of Euripides' entirely psychological approach. Of course this healing, this way out, has a limited place in the tragedies. By its very nature, tragedy studies a crisis, where no passion abates and no peace is allowed, at least till the end. Yet, there can be hints, suggesting a better course and giving birth to hope. These are of two kinds. And both take after Sophocles, but with an important shift of emphasis.

First, if everything changes, one may hope that passions can be altered too. The ideal, of course, would be a life of no passion, adapting itself to circumstances. That is more or less the supple wisdom which Sophocles intermittently advocated. Euripides follows the same line, with a hedonistic hue, which makes his evocations more personal. One passage is worth quoting: it comes from a chorus in the *Hippolytus*, and says (in Barrett's translation): "Pliant my ways, and changing them ever for the morrow's span, may I share its good fortune through my life."[40]

"Pliant my ways": this is a rule of life; it may be also a reason for hope. Indeed, if everything changes, even human feelings, why should not this very laxity provide a possibility of appeasement? In that case, the remedy will be found precisely in that which caused the suffering: in change, and in man's psychological reactions to the experience of time. For a sudden change will hurt, but long delays will heal. Sophocles used for time the verb *marainein*, meaning "to waste, to ruin, to cause to fade away." Euripides several times uses the verb *malassein*, meaning "to make soft and supple, to appease, to relieve." Two persons suggest to Admetus that time will cause his pain to abate: "Time will appease you," says Alcestis in the beginning (381: *malaxei*); and later Heracles will repeat: "Time will appease that; now your pain is attaining full growth" (1085–1087: *malaxei*). The same formula is used in the *Orestes*, of an anger that is likely to fade away: "I believe that, with time, his passion will soften" (1201: *malaxein*).

Indeed, anything can soften and fade away with time. One can forget. There is in Euripides a real philosophy of oblivion.

Oblivion heals pain. Sophocles, among others, had spo-

[40] 1117:

> *ῥᾴδια δ'ἤθεα τὸν αὔριον μεταβαλλομένα χρόνον αἰεὶ βίον συνευτυχοίην.*

ken of this oblivion of pain;[41] he had even used twice the remarkable compound *lathiponos*, "oblivious of pain;[42] but in all the cases where the idea is to be found, it always applies to a short remitment after an acute crisis.[43] In Euripides, this may be the case, just as one may seek oblivion in death.[44] Oblivion is also the natural result of time. This, of course, cannot happen within the bounds of the play. For the tragedy does not last long enough; and it leaves no room for appeasement.[45] But this faint hope always glows in the distance, as a shaky hope for later. Clytemnestra acknowledges it in the *Iphigeneia:* "Custom with time will help to make it all shrivel up and fade away,"[46] she says about the sadness of parents seeing their children leaving home.[47]

The same is true of error and anger. With time, they

[41] See also Pindar, *Ol.*, II, 17 ff., where comes λάθα, and pain dies away; but the reason for oblivion is the favor from the gods. The word λήθη is not to be found in Aeschylus.

[42] See *Ajax*, 711, and *Trach.*, 1021.

[43] To the examples mentioned above, add *Philoctetes*, 878, and fragments 238, 2 (where the cause of oblivion is a speech), and 375, 2 (where the text says: "even for a short while").

[44] For the general case, see *Orestes*, 213 (where the cause is sleep), or *Bacchae*, 282 (where it is wine); probably also fr. 342. For the oblivion in death, see *Suppliants*, 86.

[45] On the contrary, people's ancient and forgotten pains, in tragedy, are revived by the spectacle of new ones; so, in Euripides' *Electra*, 504: διὰ χρόνου σ' ἀνέμνησαν κακά.

[46] 694. There is only one verb in the Greek text, but a very powerful one: συνισχανεῖ.

[47] Oblivion is looked for, as a natural course, even in cases where the legend rules it out: in the *Phoenician Women*, it is said twice that Oedipus' sons, by locking up their father, hoped all would be forgotten (64 ff., 872 ff., where the words are συγκαλύψαι . . . χρόνῳ). See also Critias, *Incert. Fab.*, fr. 2: ὁ χρόνος ἁπάσης ἐστὶν ὀργῆς φάρμακον.

could abate. Passions are not eternal, and should not be eternal (fr. 799); time offers an opportunity for reflection and rectification. When Medea pretends that this has happened to her in the very course of the tragedy, it is, naturally, untrue; but in other times it could have been true. So, when she says she is at last abandoning her quarrel with her husband (904: *chronō(i)*), he approves: "Your heart has changed, choosing a better course, and you have found—though in the long run—the prevailing view" (912: *alla tō(i) chronō(i)*). This could have been; for anybody can change his opinions, with time; and, as Heracles says to Admetus: "The time may come when you will say I was right" (*Alcestis*, 1036: *chronō(i)*).

This explains why the tragedies of Euripides convey such an expression of interwoven urgency: with time, everything could be managed. To "allow time" is often the best course for all. In the *Ion*, the boy would like to discover his mother, the father his son's mother: well, that may come—"If we allow time, we shall perhaps succeed" (575)—and later the father explains he will not hurt his wife by telling her the truth at first; he will wait for an opportunity (659). This is the art of life. As a fragment of an unknown tragedy suggests, a good doctor allows time for the illness, which he finally cures, and does not act the surgeon too soon (fr. 1072). Sophocles' Ajax had said the contrary (*Ajax*, 581–582).

This healing power of course only glitters as the faint hope of a dispirited heart, tired at the spectacle of human passions and miseries. It is interesting to us as a sign of the utterly psychological manner in which Euripides considers time and its influence on human life. Indeed there shows, in these passages, some of the melancholy, indulging in moods and foregone emotions, which were later to grow up into poignant modern poetry. Still, if it were all the consolation Euripides could think of against the miseries of life, it would not be much.

In fact, in Euripides' theater there is another way out: another way out of time; and, as Euripides' thought is of a psychological nature, this way out of time is to be found in the psychological manner of denying time's destroying powers, that is to say, in memory.

Here again we are brought back to ideas which could be found in Sophocles. For Sophocles, when he insisted on time as discovering the truth, was certainly thinking of what men would know and remember in the future; and when his heroes chose death, as better than yielding, there was among their reasons a more or less explicit reference to the fame they would thus achieve in all men's memory.

This becomes the main justification of heroic death in Euripides. Young people, often maidens, who have no such strong personality as Ajax or Antigone, accept being sacrificed for two reasons: they have nothing good or happy to expect from life, and they can expect fame to outlast their life and misery. We can quote two particularly illuminating examples from the beginning and the end of Euripides' career as a playwright.

In the *Heraclidae*, performed soon after 430, Macaria goes willingly to death. She says first she has no hope of future happiness.[48] She explains that, were she to live, nobody would care to marry her, whereas through death she achieves the successful result of dying gloriously. The only requirement she has is to be gloriously buried (588).

[48] 520: 'Αλλ' *οὐδὲ μέντοι . . . ἐλπίδ' εὖ πράξειν ἔχω.*

The chorus gives the conclusion: "Glorious is her share in death, for her brother's sake and her country's; and the reputation she will obtain among men is not without glory" (624). She is crushed by life, so that death is the only solution left to her; but at the same time she obtains something that will outlast all the ups and downs of time, as she will be forever remembered by all.

At the very end of the Peloponnesian War and of Euripides' life, Iphigeneia will say the same, in more emphatic words. She wants to die "gloriously" (1375), and obtain "a blessed glory"; she says her help to Greece will be "her lasting monument"; it will be for her as children, wedding, and reputation. The chorus again comments: "There is no risk that glory ever fades for you"; she has provided it even for her father, who will thus obtain an "ever-remembered glory" (1531), or an "unchangeable reputation" (1606). Once more the girl could not hope for much in life; she deserved our pity and had it; yet the compensation that memory provides settles her at last in an incorruptible world.[49]

Certainly this is nothing original if we compare it with Sophocles. For his characters too, and more than any others his heroic characters, thought in terms of glory and of everlasting glory. Yet there is a difference in atmos-

[49] Similarly, Polyxena dwells sadly on the change and misery of her life, which leave her no hope; therefore she wishes for death (358: *θανεῖν ἐρᾶν*), and repeats, almost like Macaria (370–371):

οὔτ' ἐλπίδος γὰρ οὔτε του δόξης ὁρῶ
θάρσος παρ' ἡμῖν ὥς ποτ' εὖ πρᾶξαί με χρή.

She also knows she would look a coward, were she to live (348). On the contrary, Euripides lets us hear, after her death, all the complimentary comments made on the "exceptionally brave, and superior girl" (579-580).

phere and coloring. Sophoclean characters often mention renown and nobility, but they do not often insist on what will be said about them and on how long this will abide. Only Electra insists on the idea, quoting all the praise she and her sister will receive for avenging their father's murder, and adding that this will persist forever, even after their death.[50] Even there, we can detect a difference in emphasis. For what thrills Electra is the idea of achieving a heroic deed, and winning admiration as through a victory: the idea that it would last is only mentioned in the last line of about twenty lines. She is stimulated by battle and difficulty. Indeed Sophoclean characters are fighters. Antigone is a fighter. Ajax is one too. They fight in solitude, even in rebuke. On the contrary, Euripidean characters simply fly away from the miseries of life into another, more steady world. This very option, which is the background for their tender heroism, and which Sophoclean characters ignore, is Euripides' personal contribution to this classical theme.

Proof can be found in the fact that he makes similar remarks about cities, particularly about Athens. It is certainly a fact that the idea of the glorious city, of the *kleinōn Athēnōn*[51] appears in several of his plays. This would not be very original, for there is scarcely an Athenian work where the theme is not present. To mention but tragedies, it cannot be denied that Athens has pride of place in Aeschylus' *Persians* and in Sophocles' *Oedipus at Colonus.* What is worth noticing is that Euripides likes to insist both on the human and on the lasting character of this glory. He likes to show people remembering Athens'

[50] 985: *ζώσαιν θανούσαιν θ' ὥστε μὴ 'κλιπεῖν κλέος.*

[51] *Heraclidae*, 38.

generosity and giving their help through unending gratitude. For instance, we can compare Oedipus' promises in the *Oedipus at Colonus*, where he says his buried body will be a help against Theban armies because God has so decided, and Theseus' advice in the *Suppliants*, where he demands everlasting memory of Athen's help to the Argives: "You must remember these deeds and preserve their memory, seeing what you obtained from me; and you must repeat the same story to your children here, so that they shall respect our city; and one generation must hand over to the next the memory of things obtained, ever." [52] This will be the everlasting gratitude which is emphasized in the play by many powerful expressions, such as "gratitude forever" (374: *esaei*) or "gratitude unchanging with age" (1178: *agērōn*).[53] This greatness, resting on men's memory, is the decorous honor, the *agalma* (372) which makes facing any danger worth while.[54] It is obtained through pain and toil, but it remains after the pain and toil are over.[55]

Indeed that is the only manner in which time, for Euripides, means justice. In the *Andromache* a chorus says that "time does not destroy what remains from men of value; their merit shines bright, even after death. It is

[52] 1169 ff. The Greek words are very insistent: *χάριν μεμνημένους σῴζειν—μνήμην παραγγέλλοντας*.

[53] Theseus himself, in the *Heracles*, says he hates gratitude which changes with age (1223: *χάριν γηράσκουσαν*). One could also quote the promises of Iolaus in the *Heraclidae*, and his advice that Heracles' children should "remember" (314: *μεμνημένοι*).

[54] See *Heracles*, 1334–1335; *Suppliants*, 314, 561.

[55] On the numerous passages where the connection between toil and glory comes forth, see our *Thucydides and Athenian Imperialism*, pp. 134–136 of the English translation (Oxford, 1963).

better not to have an ill-famed victory than to offend justice through envy and power. For this may be at first a pleasant thing for mortals: with time, it withers away and calls for blame on one's house."[56] This is the old creed, only made logical and psychological, through words meaning praise or blame.[57] Bad behavior will bring disaster, because it will create reproach and hostility.

This mention of glory as the one everlasting thing in the human world[58] is exactly in the style and manner of Pindar. It is also very near what we find in Thucydides. Pericles, in the historian's work, says a lot about glory: that it is worth everything; that it will abide; that even after Athens has lost all her power, the memory thereof will remain forever.

The adjective *agēraos* (never-aging) is used for things in very few passages: Homer uses it for Athena's aegis; Pindar uses it for glory, but in a sentence saying that God gives it or takes it back;[59] up to the fourth century, only two authors seem to have used it of human feelings—Euripides in the *Suppliants* (with the word "gratitude") and Thucydides in the Funeral Oration (with the word "praise").

Indeed, all these beautiful adjectives and expressions

[56] 774–784. Instead of "on one's house," we should perhaps say "from other houses," or "among houses." As for "through envy and power," it would be tempting, but difficult, to understand "through a power which causes envy." This last meaning, though less natural, would be nearer to Thucydides' thought on the matter.

[57] We have here *κακόδοξον* and *ὀνείδεσι*.

[58] It recurs in many passages: see fr. 585:

> *τοῦ γὰρ δικαίου κἂν βροτοῖσι κἂν θεοῖς*
> *ἀθάνατος ἀεὶ δόξα διατελεῖ μόνου.*

[59] *Pyth.*, II, 52.

suggesting a memory lasting forever are brought forward in Thucydides. He speaks of fame (*doxa*), of unwritten memory (II. 43. 3: *agraphos mnēmē*); he speaks of the greatest of names, of a memory that will remain ever (II. 64. 3: *es aidion*), of future reputation that remains forever in the memory (II. 64. 5: *aeimnēstos*).

If we add the fact that both Euripides and Thucydides, or both Euripides' characters and Thucydides' Pericles, insist on the idea that glory is linked with toil and trouble, and makes it worth accepting them,[60] the conclusion will seem fairly obvious: we have here an echo of contemporary mood. In the difficulties of the Peloponnesian War, Athens' radiant power had to be more cherished, as its price was so high. As things seemed more threatening, it was a relief to see in them some kind of beauty that would always abide. It was Athens' answer to the hard threat of time.

That this threat and this trust were in close relation is confirmed by Thucydides, for the very sentence in which he said that memory would remain forever in future generations, is interrupted by a short parenthesis, which Euripides' pessimism would not have disclaimed: "Even if we have to give way, for everything by nature is bound to have its decline." Memory will restore what time must destroy.

Of course, Euripides remains a Greek of the fifth century and an author of tragedies. It would be absurd to ask of him that he should foreshadow all the modern evolution in thought and in art, and the modern interest in the psy-

[60] See above, p. 138 and note 55.

chology of memory. He could have written nothing even vaguely resembling either the melancholy enjoyment of the past that we find in Musset's *Souvenir*, or the acute discoveries about memory which prompted the whole work of Marcel Proust. But if these names are enough to measure the gap between Euripides and us, I think it has clearly appeared that the difference was by no means smaller between him and Aeschylus; for between one and the other, time has lost its theological dimensions to acquire psychological reality and complexity.

The result is, in a way, paradoxical. Homer had known but a fragmented and disorderly kind of time, where, as Fraenkel says, "the day" was the main notion. Then arose the idea of a continuous time, including a whole sequel of events. This idea culminated in Aeschylus' tragic time. Through Sophocles' alternate changes, we have seen time dissolving into an uncertain drift so that in Euripides "the day" again becomes all that we know. Yet there is a difference (time demands that there should be one!). This new "day" has now become tragic, precisely because it is felt as an isolated fragment of a broken *chronos*, it is not that one does not think of *chronos* as a whole, but that this *chronos* finally turns out to be irrational and to evade all human calculations. The same reason explains why the new *chronos* is now loaded with psychological pathos. For we are left with our emotions, which implies both the feeling of something amiss and the growth of new interests.

Euripides is no modern writer, but thanks to his views about time, the way has been opened to modern psychology.

6 *Young and old in Greek tragedy*

We have tried to show that a deep and thorough evolution had taken place from Aeschylus to Euripides regarding their views about time. As a confirmation, we shall now endeavor to see whether the same evolution can be traced in their views about age.

At first sight, this might be doubted. The difference between old and young people, in their merits and shortcomings, and in the happiness or unhappiness of their status, seems to be one about which everybody should agree. Indeed the description of the different ages in life has been given as something classical and obvious by several ancient writers, the best-known of all being Horace.[1] Yet even in these well-established features and commonplace ideas, each author can choose, according to his own idea about the effects of time. If the general view is the same, the emphasis changes, from one to the other. The

[1] See also, in ancient Greek texts, Hesiod, fr. 220 Rz.; Solon, [27], 3 H; Democritus, A, 294 Diels.

study of these different choices ought to confirm what we have seen about the evolution of ideas from Aeschylus to Euripides; it may also provide a closer approach to its meaning, and, thereby, a general conclusion to our present research.

❖

For Aeschylus, things are easy. With him, there is no problem. As time's action, in his work, is mainly an enlightning one—time teaching lessons—it is obvious that with age comes wisdom: nothing, apparently, could prevent his old men from being wise and respectable, or his young men from being imprudent.

From the lessons of time, old men have primarily learned justice. A fragment of a lost tragedy says it quite clearly: "Old age has a better sense of justice than youth (fr. 400 N). Indeed an old man will generally be reasonable and reliable in Aeschylus' plays. In the *Suppliants*, the old father, advocating prudence, reminds his daughters that he himself is a prudent adviser: "You have come here under the guidance of your old father, who is a prudent, reliable man." [2] Indeed, respecting what is ancient, respecting one's own parents, is equal to respecting the gods, fathers of all creatures (especially mythical creatures, of divine ancestry): in the *Suppliants*, again, the honors due to the gods are justified by the mention that "to worship one's parents is the third law inscribed in the book of Justice, most honored of all" (707).

As a matter of fact, it would be easy to show that in most of Aeschylus' plays, old people act as wise counci-

[2] 177: φρονοῦντι . . . πιστῷ γέροντι.

lors, whose advice should never be overlooked. This makes them ideal members of choruses. For they are, by nature, less apt for action and more apt for understanding. Hence comes their function, which often is to guess, feel, or understand, better than the characters, the true meaning of what is going on. This is quite obvious in two plays where the chorus is made up of old men and much stress is laid on their age: first, the most ancient play we have, the *Persians*, then one of the latest in Aeschylus' career, the *Agamemnon*. In both, the chorus is made up of the men who were too old to go to war and are left behind, to wait for the issue. In the *Persians*, they are, more specifically, the king's old advisers, a sort of privy council, whose members are officially called the trusty councilors. Everyone is careful to add to this official qualification the mention of their great age. In her first address to them, in line 171, Queen Atossa calls them "old and faithful men"; and when King Darius comes back from among the dead, his first greeting is for the "faithful among the faithful, the people of his age, eldest in Persia."[3] The "eldest" not only are treated as wise councilors by the king and queen; they also display, in their reflections, a deep insight into the inner nature of things. From the very beginning they know they have cause to worry—not only because time passes and there is no news, but because they feel there was something insolent and almost impious in the whole enterprise. It was an army sent for destroying cities, that began with a daring action against the majesty of the divine sea, an action which might well be the sign of a fatal delusion, foreboding a just disaster. As the news of

[3] 681–682:

> *ὦ πιστὰ πιστῶν ἥλικές θ' ἥβης ἐμῆς*
> *Πέρσαι γεραιοί.*

this disaster comes forth, the old men are quite entitled to draw the difference between right and wrong behavior and to comment upon the heavy blow sent by divine justice (852 ff.).

Similarly, in the *Agamemnon*, the old men of Argos are apt to grasp what was wrong from the start in the fleet's departure, and to detect a fault likely to bring out disaster. As news reaches the palace, they can point to the manifestation of divine justice and foresee worse events yet to come, according to the same justice.[4]

This moral and intellectual superiority is no doubt a result of their very age and experience. It shows the true merit of age.

Does it mean that age is altogether an advantage and superiority? It would be absurd to pretend so. Aeschylus was just as capable as Homer, or as anybody else, of seeing the destructive influence of age, and of complaining about it. These very old men of Argos, in the *Agamemnon*, regret that they have lost their strength, and cannot fight any more. They state their weakness in powerful words, at their first appearance: their old body prevents them from fighting with the others and they have to use a stick in order to help their strength, which is like a child's (*isopaida*). They even combine Homeric or lyric images in order to describe this decaying influence: "What is a very old man, when life's foliage withers? He walks on three legs, no better than a child, and wanders about like an empty dream in day-light": [5] this comparison

[4] The most relevant lines are 105 ff., 367 ff., 681 ff., 975 ff.

[5] *Agamemnon*, 72–83; the line about withering leaves recalls Archilochus, 113 D. It will be noted that here we have "excessive" age: ὑπέργηρως.

of old people with children recurs in the *Eumenides:* "A frightened old woman is nothing: indeed no more than a child." [6]

But, unlike other authors, Aeschylus always insists that this physical decay does not touch the soul or brain. The old men of the *Agamemnon* are glad that at least they can sing about the foreboding events which happened ten years ago: thanks to the gods their age still inspires them, and persuasion is left to them.[7] Nor is this exceptional: for we find many an example, in the other plays, of old men being wise, even though their physical strength may be gone. In the *Suppliants*, Danaus says he will not deserve any reproach as an ambassador: he is "an old man, yet a young one for his mind and good speech." [8] In the *Seven against Thebes* there is a similar contrast, which might even lead to misunderstanding; the poet speaks of a man who is "old as regards his mind, but owns a youthful body." [9] In any other author, one might imagine that the first part of the line suggests some criticism, as if the man lacked intellectual dynamism; but, here, it is obviously a compliment: the man combines the perfection of both intellectual wisdom and physical power.

Therefore, only villains can be rude to old men; only villains can want to make them wiser, as does Aegisthus

[6] 38: *δείσασα γὰρ γραῦς οὐδέν· ἀντίπαις μὲν οὖν.*

[7] 106–107. The exact translation is discussed, but the general meaning is clear. It is interesting to notice that Euripides has a parallel passage in the *Heracles*, 678, but that, characteristically enough, the possibility of explaining things has been replaced, with him, by the possibility of practicing art and of celebrating Memory!

[8] 774–775: *γέρονθ' ἡβῶντα δ' εὐγλώσσῳ φρενί.*

[9] 622: *γέροντα τὸν νοῦν, σάρκα δ' ἡβῶσαν φέρει.*

toward the end of the *Agamemnon*.[10] As for themselves, they never bewail or even deplore their general condition.[11] Indeed, old men enjoy wisdom, which is the highest good in human life.

Now the wisdom of age has a counterpart. If old men are wise, young men are not; and we actually find Aeschylus dwelling on the gross folly of young people.

The clearest example is, of course, Xerxes. As Darius explains, Xerxes did not know; he acted on youth's bold rashness (*Persians*, 744: *neō(i) thrasei*). He could scarcely do otherwise, being a youngster: "My son Xerxes, being a young man, has the thoughts of a young man, and he forgets about my advice." Therefore, the only hope for him is that his insolence should be tempered with old people's admonition: Darius tells the old queen and the "eldest": "Let your wise remonstrances correct him, so that he stops offending the gods by his arrogant boldness" (829–831).

If we transfer the scene from human to divine beings, we shall find similar ideas in the *Prometheus*, about young gods and their imprudent pride. Not only is Zeus' power a young power,[12] but he himself has not yet learned wis-

[10] 1619: *γνώσῃ γέρων ὢν ὡς διδάσκεσθαι βαρύ*. That an old man can still learn is a possibility that Solon knew and Aeschylus elsewhere admits; but it is a possibility worth some admiration, as old men have already learned so much (cf. fr. 396: *καλὸν δὲ καὶ γέροντι μανθάνειν σοφά*).

[11] The *Persians* provides only one hint: the old men have lived too long, if they have lived to learn such news (264–265). But only the common disaster explains this regret, not their age in itself.

[12] This is mentioned in lines 149, 310, 389, 942, 960. But it should be noted that the idea is not very different from what we are dealing with now: a new power means, as youth itself, lack of experience, of wisdom, and of justice.

dom; and he thinks, like Xerxes, that he can do anything: "Being young, you hold a young power, and you apparently think you live in a castle impervious to pain" (955). The young god Zeus is not altogether different from the young king Xerxes.[13]

But here a problem seems to arise. Indeed, there is another of Aeschylus' plays where mention is made of "young" gods, and of their undue ambition. That is the *Eumenides*, where the Furies never stop attacking the new generation of gods, represented by Apollo and Athena. Between them, a conflict of generations seems to open before us. "Such are the ways of these younger gods" complain the old deities; "They hold full power more than justice allows," or later: "Being young, you trample under foot my old age," or again: "Ah, younger gods, you trample under foot ancient laws."[14] Athena herself insists on their prerogatives, for she will not have it said by anyone that as a young goddess (882: *neōteras*) she has banished an ancient one (*palaia*).

Precisely this reticence provides an answer to our question. Athena will not have it said. And she acts in such manner that it will never be said. She is patient, obstinate, polite. She is even kind and deferent—so much so that, in the end, everybody comes to an agreement. The old

13 In the *Seven against Thebes*, Eteocles is, in the beginning, very proud and superior in scolding the women of the chorus; but when he yields to his father's curse, his youthful passion is immediately contrasted with the women's experience: 686, *τί μέμονας, τέκνον*. From that very minute, the relation between him and the chorus changes: the chorus is henceforward gifted with high understanding and wisdom, as in the *Agamemnon*.

14 See lines 162–163, 731, and 808.

Furies become benevolent; the young goddess promises that they will be honored. Young and old are reconciled and prepare the future together.[15] Even when the younger generation is represented by Athena and Apollo, it cannot be allowed to overlook old age. And even when the Furies' cruelty sounds the most archaic, nothing is apt to overrule their privilege. For they can claim the title of all that is ancient and noble: the words meaning "ancient," "old," "antique" always sound favorable in Aeschylus' poetry.

Indeed the majesty of age seems to have been then so well rooted in Greek thought and habits that one could almost wonder at its ever having been questioned. Yet, it was questioned soon after, and Greek tragedy shows us how.

Not that Sophocles ever lacked respect for old age. Just as we have found in his plays several conventional statements about divine justice, we can find in them polite remarks about the wisdom of old men—at least we find them in the fragments of lost tragedies, where moralizing collectors of quotations selected them for us: [16] in

[15] Something similar was probably to be found in the last play of the trilogy about Prometheus. In any case, a like agreement between human generations is achieved when we hear, in the *Persians*, of the advice Xerxes will get from the elders.

[16] The fragments to be quoted are: 239 N, 260 P ("intelligence and correct decisions generally are companions of old age"); 603 N, 664 P ("old age teaches one all, with the experience of time"); 864 N, 950 P (about wise men never getting old, whose intelligence fulfills certain rules, not quite clear in the text as we have it). See also 194 N, 193 P.

fact, none of them actually exists in the extant plays.[17]

What stands out is something that scarcely ever appeared in Aeschylus: people complain of age. More interested in man himself than in the causes of his fate, Sophocles tends to show how all these changes that occur under the influence of time are hard and sad to bear. Twice in his tragedies, there are grown-up people, affected by all they have gone through, who look back with melancholy to the tender ignorance of youth. Deianeira thus looks back to the protected peace of the unmarried girl. She wishes that the lessons of age should not come too quickly, for they come with suffering.[18] Indeed, "what is young grows up in such regions of its own as to ignore this experience: it suffers no heat from the heavenly sun, nor rain, nor any raging wind; it lives without trouble, enjoying pleasure, till comes the time when. . . ." And Ajax, after the total overthrow he has suffered, turns with envy to his young child: "I can envy you in this," he says, "that you have no notions of those miseries. It's before you can use sense that life is most pleasurable."[19]

This twin, melancholy remembrance of the sweetness of youth is complemented by a well-known lament on the sadness of age: it is the famous lyrics in the *Oedipus at*

[17] In the *Coloneus*, 7–8, there is a mention about age teaching patience (στέργειν). Otherwise, we can find mention of people developing reflection (φῦναι φρένας), but the expression is often used by rough tyrants, who think of using violence (*Oed. Col.*, 805, and, with still more certainty, *Electra*, 1463).

[18] 143: μήτ' ἐκμάθοις παθοῦσα: this is the old πάθει μάθος of Aeschylus, but seen from the angle of pointless suffering.

[19] This is line 554. In the following lines, Ajax suggests, like Deianeira, the idea of some tenderly growing plant: "Till then, feed on light breezes and foster your young life, for your mother's joy."

Colonus, where, with no specific reason, the old Sophocles suddenly dwells on the misery of being old.[20] He says that it is folly to wish for a long life: "For the long days do offer many things which come nearer to sorrow; delightful ones you could not find, once you have lapsed beyond what was suitable." [21] And once more Sophocles declares that youth is the only happy moment, "youth with its light inconscience." [22] After that, nothing but pain: "envy, factions, quarrel, battles and murders, and, for the end, dispraised old age, with no force, no sociable life, no friends,[23] where all the worst of woes gather together." In this regret, one can hear the echo of Sophocles' own taste for happy life and gentle society. No doubt lyric poets had complained about age before,[24] and Euripides' tragedies—which are almost all to be placed before the *Oedipus at Colonus*—did acclimatize such themes in tragedy; yet, the feeling is personal, and the poetry so powerful as not to leave any doubt about the deepness of the impact.[25]

[20] 1211 ff. Oedipus, no doubt, is old; but nobody could pretend that his miseries were caused by age. G. M. Kirkwood has, in fact, insisted on the contrast between the despairing gloom of this song and the vigor and power of spirit displayed by Oedipus in what follows (*A Study of Sophoclean Drama* [Ithaca, 1958], p. 201).

[21] Sophocles even declares that death is then the happiest solution: see also *Ajax*, 473, and Theognis, 425.

[22] ἀφροσύνας: the word echoes φρονεῖν in the *Ajax*.

[23] These adjectives remind one of a similar list in Aeschylus; only—and this is characteristic enough—in Aeschylus, it applied not to age, but to war, or, more exactly, to Ares: ἄχορον, ἀκίθαριν, δακρυόγονον (*Supp.*, 681).

[24] See below, p. 159.

[25] See also 512 N, 556 P: "There is no such misery as a long life."

Sophocles knew that old age was distasteful. And he knew that time, which introduces so much change in human circumstances, also introduces some change in man's feelings and in his mind.

In fact, old age, for him, does not mean only the loss of physical strength. With him, we have to open a new chapter about age: an old man loses also his intelligence and wisdom. One might be betrayed by age; and, when consulted on a difficult topic, the members of the chorus in the *Antigone* suggest they may be too old to judge: "To us, if our years don't deceive us, you seem to speak wisely on the things you speak of" (681–682). Several fragments go even further, suggesting various shortcomings, all attached to old age;[26] the most decisive of all is fragment 863 N (949 P), where it is said that "all miseries are by nature attached to great age"; and the passage goes on: "Intelligence is gone, acts have no effect, intentions are empty."[27] That even one's intelligence might suffer is in accordance with what we read in Herodotus about the soul losing its force and edge;[28] and it will be re-

[26] Fragment 63 N, 66 P says nobody is as eager to live as the aging man. Was this a criticism or not? In any case it leads to Euripides' criticism (see below, p. 165). Fragment 447 N, 487 P says that the aging man has returned to childhood: this is certainly applied to physical strength, but it does not sound utterly respectful. Fragment 808 N, 894 P says that an old man's anger quickly loses its force: that could be complimentary, but points to a change in character, which is altogether alarming.

[27] *νοῦς φροῦδος, ἔργ' ἀχρεῖα, φρόντιδες κεναί.*

[28] Atossa tells Darius to try some great deed while he is still young: "For the soul, which grows up with the body, also grows old with it; and it loses its strength for doing anything" (III, 134). The verb *ἀμβλύνονται* is the same one used by Sophocles in fragment 808 N, 894 P, quoted above, in note 26.

membered that Herodotus and Sophocles had much in common. On the other hand, this idea is widely different from anything that could be found in Aeschylus.

The consequences are easy to see: for, as a result, we can now have unreasonable old men. In the *Antigone*, Creon warns the leader of the chorus that he should take care not to turn out to be "at the same time foolish and old."[29] These adjectives are not of similar trend, but of contrasting meaning; and "at the same time" suggests that it is particularly scandalous to be still foolish in spite of one's old age. A similar scandal and similar reproach recurs in the *Oedipus at Colonus*, where Creon, this time, scolds Oedipus himself: "O wretched man, even with time will you never acquire brains? You are a shame to old age" (804–805). By a nice kind of poetic justice, Creon also is blamed by Theseus in comparable language; for Theseus says that increasing years make him "at the same time old and empty-minded."[30] All these isolated remarks hint at the same idea. Old age should be wise: but it is often seen not to obey that law.

Hence a problem, for now the privilege of age is less justified: it can be questioned. It can be denied. And conflicts may arise. Old men are not necessarily wiser than young ones. Indeed, there may be in youth some fresh and brave honesty, which can be preferred to the rash authority of older people. A man who claims obedience in no other capacity than the privilege of age may be quite in the wrong.

Sophocles seems to have been greatly impressed with

[29] 281: *ἄνους τε καὶ γέρων ἅμα.*

[30] 930: *γέρονθ' ὁμοῦ τίθησι καὶ τοῦ νοῦ κενόν.*

the notion that there is a special kind of behavior adapted for each kind of age. Antigone in the *Oedipus at Colonus* should not, *at her age*, speak too long; she should not, *at her age*, live as she does.[31] In the same tragedy, Creon often mentions his own age, which prepares him to be a pacific and wise ambassador.[32] In the *Antigone*, he is not yet so old (nor is Sophocles); yet he is indignant at the idea of having to listen to his son's advice: "Are we going to receive lessons *at our age* from a boy *of such age* in life?" (726). Clytemnestra, in the *Electra*, is no less indignant at her daughter's disrespectful attitude: Electra should not speak to her mother as she does, especially *at her age;*[33] and Electra herself admits that this is "untimely" of her.

All this shows quite clearly that a problem has arisen; it also shows where Sophocles' sympathy lies. Those who claim the rights of age as a sheer rule of authority are Creon and Clytemnestra—rather suspicious warrants! It is easy to see that, where a discussion arises, he takes sides with the younger heroes, who advocate other standards. Electra would like to be a respectful daughter in a normal life; she has no personal taste for murder or even action; but she has no choice. She is of heroic nature and knows that she must fight: "Be well assured that I feel ashamed, even if you don't think so. . . . But your own hostility and your deeds compel me to act in that way, in spite of what I wish." Against Clytemnestra's villainy, she stands

[31] In the first passage, the idea is "being so young"; here, it means: "being old enough to be married."

[32] 735. Yet he is capable of action, even at his age (959: καὶ τηλικόσδ' ὤν).

[33] 614. In all the examples quoted here, we have either τηλικοῦτος or τηλικόσδε.

out as an image of incorruptible righteousness. A young creature can therefore, if her nature is noble, know from the very start what is good and worthy. It could even be suggested that for such a young creature this instinctive knowledge is more natural than for older people, lost in the greed and rancor of their own private interests. Yet Sophocles does not go that far. He does not say it; he only emphasizes this startling reversal of things.

The same situation is also to be found in the *Antigone.* The young people again are right, and, again, because they have spontaneously chosen the highest standards and absolute values. Haemon is a respectful son. He insists on his regard for his father, even in his first words: "Father, I am yours; your wise advice is a rule for me, which I follow. No marriage will be of more value to me than your noble guidance." [34] Creon at first rejoices in such docility. But Haemon, in spite of all his respect, is unbending, because he knows he is right and gives good advice. Therefore he comes to say himself: "If indeed I am young, you must not look at my years, but at my behavior." [35] He speaks for justice, and for reason. Creon, carried by his pride and love of power, speaks as if he were blinded by youth (735: "as a man too young"). One could declare that he is corrupted by power; Sophocles only shows that the elder here acts with less wisdom than his very son.

Antigone and Haemon are both young, both sure of

[34] This in lines 635 ff.; see also, later, 685 ff., 701 ff., 755.

[35] This is to be found in lines 728–729. Cf. Corneille:

> "Je suis jeune, il est vrai, mais aux âmes bien nées
> La valeur n'attend pas le nombre des années."

what is right, both ready to follow their ideas at the price of their lives. Their revolt is heroism.

Indeed, there is in Sophocles' theater another very young man who revolts in heroism. There the situation is even more startling. Neoptolemus is young and he is told to obey Odysseus, against his own natural feeling. Odysseus has become wise with age and thinks it fit to lie sometimes; he explains: "I also was young, once, . . . but now . . ." (96 ff.). Neoptolemus first obeys. Later, his true instinct and natural righteousness suddenly burst forth and he chooses revolt, with uncompromising certainty, even though he may lose everything in life.

Nowhere do we read that these young people, whom their elders affectionately call "child," are heroic because they are young; but it is fairly obvious that their whole tragedy arises from having to act, in spite of their youth and frailty, against the world's powers, and from being, all of them, such exemplary exceptions to the superiority of age.

In fact, all this illustrates in a very clear fashion the existence of a new trend of thought. Sophocles, no doubt, does not follow it avowedly or consciously: he never takes sides with youth as such against old age as such. But his choice, although it does not lead to any general conclusion, is always in favor of noble and uncompromising young people against their blind and ambitious elders. His very facts proclaim a new approach to age, which is directly connected with the new approach to time showing in his tragedies. Time, for him, is no more a teaching power, the good influence of which made the old wise: it is a threatening and destructive power; and its bad influence can only be overcome by the strength and nobleness of man's natural qualities.

✣ ✣ ✣

It will not, then, be a surprise that this destructive power of time is even more strongly emphasized in Euripides' plays—some of which, it will be remembered, were older than Sophocles' plays.

But of course we find in Euripides' plays the traditional view also. We have already seen some examples showing that time can teach a useful lesson: this is the case in casual, proverbial remarks which we hear from the nurse in the *Hippolytus:* "Long life teaches me a lot of things" (252), or from the herald in the *Suppliants:* "Time affords a better lesson than hurry" (419). It recurs in the first words of Jocasta about the advantage of age, which is experience.[36] The same idea also inspires several fragments about the wisdom of old age, where we find mention of the "lesson," or of the "mind" and "judgment," always contrasted with the physical strength of youth.[37]

[36] *Phoenician Women*, 528–530.

[37] Three fragments are to be mentioned—namely, in Nauck:

291: *ὦ παῖ, νέων τοι δρᾶν μὲν ἔντονοι χέρες,*
γνῶμαι δ' ἀμείνους εἰσὶ τῶν γεραιτέρων.
ὁ γὰρ χρόνος δίδαγμα ποικιλώτατον.

508: *ἔργα μὲν νεωτέρων*
βουλαὶ δ' ἔχουσι τῶν γεραιτέρων κράτος.

619: *τὸ γῆρας, ὦ παῖ, τῶν νεωτέρων φρενῶν*
σοφώτερον πέφυκε κἀσφαλέστερον,
ἐμπειρία τε τῆς ἀπειρίας κρατεῖ.

It is also probable that fragment 510, where a man is said to be *νέος καὶ σκαιός*, points out the imprudent rashness of youth.

These are only isolated remarks, never much expanded or borne out by the general trend of the plays.

Passages about the misery of old age are on the whole more personal. This is specially true of the sad song in the *Heracles* (637 ff.). This song is quite as remarkable as the one in the *Oedipus at Colonus;* it is not more closely related to the general theme, nor less passionate. But two differences can be detected.[38] First, whereas Sophocles' song is general, Euripides' is individually sentimental. Sophocles indeed considers man's happiness; but his analysis speaks about "man"; and only toward the end does he bring in a personal word saying: "This is Oedipus' fate, not mine alone." All Euripides says is "I like," "I don't like," "I hate." His point of view is lyrical, his universe centered on individual feelings.[39] Secondly, whereas Sophocles, always remaining in touch with human problems and answers, sees in death the one remedy for all, Euripides dwells on impossible wishes and dreams of a perpetual youth. This tendency shows from beginning to end. Thus when he says: "Youth is for me the ever beloved age. Old age, on the other hand, weighs on my head, heavier than Mt. Etna; and it hangs before my eyes as a dark veil. I should not wish either the luxury of the kingdom of Asia, or a palace filled with gold, were it to be instead of youth—for youth is so beautiful in luxury, so beautiful also in poverty! But the sad old age, which

[38] It is true that the men of the chorus are old, and that age makes them helpless; but there are many other reasons explaining the impending disaster, which could just as well be commented upon.

[39] See expressions like 637: *μοι φίλον—ἄχθος*; 642: *μή μοι* . . . ; 650: *μισῶ*. It is easy to quote parallels for the theme in Simonides or Mimnermus (see Mimnermus, fr. 1–5).

kills you, this I hate! May it disappear under the waves, may it vanish away from the houses and cities of men, where it should never have come, and be carried away in the air, in an everlasting flight!"

This passionate stanza, with its exclamations of hatred and refusal, is of such inner sharpness that it is in itself more convincing than all the casual remarks one could pick up here and there. So many passages echo it in Euripides' theater that the combination of them all adds to the weight of the evidence. The old Iphis, in the *Suppliants*, uses the same expression of hatred (*misō*, "I hate") for old age: "O hard wrestler, you, old age, how I hate your presence!"[40] This is also the tone in numerous fragments—I do not mean the objective ones, like fragment 575, line 3, which says: "Long age gives birth to numberless pains"; I mean the exclamative or affective ones, which are all perfectly concordant: old age is "bitter" in fragment 282; fragment 637 exclaims about the "illnesses" or miseries it brings; fragment 805 explains about the "evil" it is; fragment 453 speaks of it as undoing man's possibilities with its "pains"; fragment 1080 sarcastically remarks that everybody wishes to live a long life, but regrets it once old, "for there is nothing worse than old age."[41]

All these statements constitute a bitter lament, appearing here and there, all through Euripides' work, as if of people pathetically intent on their own suffering.

Among these regrets, which age inspires, will naturally emerge the idea that old people lose everything, even their former qualities. In a way, one acquires experience.

[40] 1108. See also, in the same play, 1118–1119.

[41] The words quoted translate πικρόν, νόσους, κακόν, πόνοις.

But what else is not destroyed, whether physical, or intellectual, or moral?

The loss of physical strength is not new, but it is pathetically emphasized. Old people in Euripides are unable to act, unable to walk, unable to stand. They can try, but it is of no avail. The chorus tells Iolaus in the *Heraclidae* (702 ff.) that, if his spirit is still young, his body "is gone"; and then adds: "Why do you take useless pains, harming yourself while you are of small help to our city? Old age must change feelings and dismiss what is out of reach: there is no possibility of recovering youth again."[42] Many of Euripides' old men, confronted with such physical failure, address their own limbs in sorrow, seeing that these refuse their services: "Ah, my old legs!" they exclaim, with either a wish that they could be rejuvenated or a regret that they cannot be.[43] Old people seem to have been worn out, by suffering as well as by age:[44] "Take these, servants of the weak old woman," says the chorus in the *Suppliants* (1118), "she has no strength left, thus mourning her children's death: she has lived for a long time and is consuming herself in numerous woes."

But physical strength is not the only loss. With physical strength goes love. Euripides several times mentions the sad condition of old men as regards love and marriage.[45] Even their wisdom is easily doubted: "How could

[42] This is again the powerless condition (*ἀμηχανία*) of one who lives in impossible wishes (recovering youth would be the negation of time).

[43] See *Ion*, 1042: *ὦ γεραιὲ πούς, νεανίας γενοῦ | ἔργοισι κεἰ μὴ τῷ χρόνῳ πάρεστί σοι*. See also 876.

[44] Both seem to be tied together by a sort of necessary connection.

[45] See fr. 23 (*ἥ τ' Ἀφροδίτη τοῖς γέρουσιν ἄχθεται*), frs. 804 and 807 (about the old husband and his young wife).

one still ascribe wisdom to old men?" asks Menelaus, in line 645 of the *Andromache*. Even old men complain: "We have no wits, we only imagine that we are wise" (fr. 25).

But there is not much point in trying to classify all the losses of old age: in short, it means complete ruin. Here it may be interesting to see what use Euripides has made of the one powerful formula which we have found in Aeschylus. Complaining of their physical weakness, the old men of the *Agamemnon* had said that the very old man "walks on three legs, no better than a child, and wanders about like an empty dream in daylight."[46] This empty dream, this *onar* seems to have haunted Euripides' thought; we find it repeated and amplified in quite a number of tragedies. In the *Heraclidae* an old man is brutally called "a tomb, a nothing";[47] in the *Heracles*, the old men come in leaning on their sticks and singing sadly as a white-feathered swan, and they add: "I am but words, and the mere appearance of dreams in the dark of the night":[48] these are Aeschylus' words, only so strongly emphasized as to leave us with the impression of complete illusion and unreality. This impression is made even more precise in the *Trojan Women* (192 ff.), where Hecuba complains that she is a wretched old woman, useless as a drone, "miserable shape of a dead being, powerless image from among the dead." It recurs in the *Phoenician Women*, where Oedipus says he is "a phantasm appearing in the air, or a phantom from the underworld, or a winged

[46] See above, p. 146.

[47] 167: *τύμβου, τὸ μηδὲν ὄντος.*

[48] 107: *δόκημα νυκτερωπὸν ἐννύχων ὀνείρων.*

dream."[49] It recurs in a fragment of the *Aeolus* (fr. 25), where old people approve what, they say, is an ancient idea about them: "We old men are nothing but mere noise and appearance: we crawl along as imitations of dreams." It recurs in fewer words in a fragment of the *Melanippe:* "What else? an old man is a voice and a shadow" (509: *phōnē kai skia*). The powerless condition of age, suggested by one line in Aeschylus (and perhaps others in lost poetry too), could not be put forward in a more obstinate or a more startling way.

That such feeling is not just easy and traditional pathos is confirmed by what we find in the plays themselves.

All Euripides' plays offer a long procession of miserable, powerless, complaining old people, crouching in agony and despair. In the first plays, Euripides seems to have sometimes pitied them enough to offer them a later compensation, but not without dwelling a long time on their previous incapacity. As early as the *Heraclidae*, we see old Iolaus, brutally treated because he is helpless: "See this old man, lying on the ground, where he has been thrown down, poor wretch!" (75–76). He offers his life in order to save Heracles' children; but even his life has no more value: "What would Eurystheus gain, with an old man's death?" (466). He cannot help in battle; he knows he is weak: "We are an old man," he says, "and have no strength at all"; the others know it as well: "Your body is no more . . . ; you won't ever recover youth" (703 ff.). Toward the end, in a long and useless scene, Euripides shows us Iolaus starting for the battle by a

[49] 1545: *αἰθεροφανὲς εἴδωλον ἢ νέκυν ἔνερθεν ἢ πτανὸν ὄνειρον.*

sheer miracle of will to meet finally with a real miracle: "From an old man, he has been transformed once more into a young one" (797). This miracle, which is a rare thing in Euripides' theater, is characteristic enough: it is the one miracle that everybody longs to experience, and that redeems all other miseries.

In the *Andromache*, we are confronted with another old man who finally achieves something. But this time the miracle is Menelaus' cowardice. For Peleus is old. His "old foot" is mentioned as soon as he is seen arriving (546). He needs help in walking (747), and Andromache is afraid lest his age will encourage his enemies to attack them. But Menelaus is weak; he remarks that old men are impossible to manage with their sharp angers and promptly retires. Nor does Peleus think Menelaus will make an attack: he trusts his own force: "I am still straight, not the old man you think, and with such an adversary, a simple glance will mean victory, whatever my age: there are many young men whom an old man, if brave, is likely to surpass" (761 ff.). This, surely, is exceptional bravery on the one hand, exceptional cowardice on the other. And the pathos of Peleus' age enhances both.

But generally old men are not victorious.

In the *Heracles*, there is strong emphasis on Amphitryon's helpless situation, and also on the age of his friends, the members of the chorus. Amphitryon is constantly addressed, by all, as "old man"; [50] and the chorus is similarly addressed.[51] The first song of the chorus is to complain about old age, and there is a realistic description of the

[50] 60, 81, 514, 1045, 1068, 1165, 1404, 1418.

[51] 275.

difficulty they find in the simple activity of moving about: "Do not let your feet and limbs tire too soon . . . ; take hold of the hands and coat of whoever has lost the fragile strength of his foot; let one old man help another" (119ff.). And again they should like to fight, but they know they are unable to do as they wish, "because of their weakness." They can only mourn their old age in another song: "If only I had the strength of youth and could brandish the spear in battle with other young men of Thebes, I should stand in front of these children, with all my power; but I am now bereft of happy youth" (436 ff.). This time salvation again comes, but not through rejuvenation.

In the *Suppliants*, the theme is again similar, for the old Adrastus is found crouching on the ground, with women and children. He speaks on their behalf, but says he is ashamed to kneel on the floor and seize Theseus' hand, being a formerly happy king, whose hair has grown white (165–166).

As for old Hecuba, her age and grief mingle in the intense pathos of both the *Hecuba* and the *Trojan Women*.[52]

But Euripides' old people are not only miserable and weak. If we think of the *Alcestis*, we soon see that they can be weak even from a moral point of view. As Sophocles says in a lost tragedy, old people are attached to life; and it is well known that to be "attached to life" (*philopsuchein*), was mean and faulty. Euripides in the *Alcestis* has put great emphasis on the father's refusal to die for the sake of saving his son;[53] and he has insisted, that such

[52] On this pathos, see our *L'évolution du pathétique, d'Eschyle à Euripide* (Paris, 1961), pp. 80–82.

[53] This scene may well have been Euripides' own invention.

refusal is a shocking but not surprising consequence of old age: "It is apparently in vain that old men call for death, complaining of age and of a too long life: when death approaches, nobody wants to die, and age is no more a burden."[54] Later in the play, Admetus will say: "I saw that you were striving after a long life." Certainly he is far from right when he reproaches his father with a cowardice that resembles his own. All the same, the father's egoism is very powerfully shown and denounced. Old people's wisdom seems to have become the mean wisdom of looking after one's self, and choosing one's own interest.

This is all the more remarkable as Euripides offers us a whole gallery of very young people who die with generosity, easiness, and nobleness. They do not take arms against opposition or fight their own fight in loneliness, like Sophocles' girls and young men: they are threatened with death and choose to accept it willingly. Alcestis does so, who is younger than Pheres; but still, she is a married woman and a mother. Macaria in the *Heraclidae* is practically a child; but, confronted with death, she suddenly discloses the courage of an adult and the wisdom which used to be that of old age.[55] Polyxena, in the *Hecuba*, is perhaps more grown up; still, she is an unmarried girl, a "filly"; and her acceptance of death sounds clear and pure against the rhetoric of older people. Her death joins courage and grace in a most lovely manner. So Iphigeneia's

[54] 699 ff. We naturally find, once more, the *γηραιῷ ποδί* (611).

[55] This appears in her *ultima verba*, 574 ff. Compare fragment 344, saying that a young man can indeed, even at his age, have acquired intellectual experience through suffering: *νέος, πόνοις δέ γ' οὐκ ἀγύμναστος φρένας*.

courage will later be conspicuous against her parents passions, and shine as a sort of grace, glowing with newly acquired pride. Menoeceus, in the *Phoenician Women*, is just as young, perhaps younger; he is a "colt"; and his decision similarly stands out against his father's sharp refusal. He is a sweet, idealistic youngster. And we know that, even when they were not required to die, such sweet, idealistic youngsters were not rare in Euripides' theater. Hippolytus may be overvirtuous, but he is a sweet, idealistic youngster; and Ion, who is even younger, is even sweeter and more idealistic. His purity has been preserved by religious life, and he does not know any other feeling than the joy of living on the gods' happy premises, away from all evil; when recognized as the son of a king, he shrinks from any power that means fear and suspicion. In fact, Ion's virtue explains the other young people's heroism in Euripides' theater: his virtue, like their heroism, arises from the fact that they are pure, untouched, and unpolluted by the experience of age.

One could add still other evidence, and mention Euripides' children, more touching in their grief than any adults: they linger about in almost every play as the nostalgic dream of tender innocence. As it is, the evidence is thoroughly convincing: Euripides' theater dwells systematically on the miseries of age, on the charms and virtues of youth.

This conclusion would therefore be enough—but for one fact: that in some plays Euripides not only reminds us of the wisdom of age but curiously insists on the imprudence of youth, even when no necessity invites him to do it. Why, in such cases, this recurrence of what might be called the Xerxes-theme?

The question is of interest, as there seems to have been, at the time, a question—a social and political question of youth against elderly people. Partly, perhaps, with the evolution in the idea of time, largely, no doubt, under the influence of democratic ideas, and later of war, young men in Athens had acquired independence and importance. They had started a new era, when respect of parents and elders was not so much the fashion. They had their own way. The quickness of the evolution in all things made them sure they were in the right. I should think this is a state of things not altogether impossible for us to understand. Proof of it is afforded by the *Clouds* of Aristophanes, for instance. And it seems pretty certain that after Pericles' death, youth took sides with the new leaders, who were for imperialism, against people like Nicias, who were for moderation. Thucydides, indeed, has turned the discussion between Nicias and Alcibiades, before the Sicilian expedition, into a discussion between young and old.[56] It should be noticed that the plays where the wisdom of age is recalled are also those where we find surprising digressions about the imprudence of youth, namely the *Hippolytus*, the *Andromache*, and most of all, the *Suppliants*, three plays probably written between 428 and 420 (between Pericles' death and the Sicilian expedition—precisely the same epoch when Aristophanes' *Clouds* was performed[57]). In the *Hippolytus*, it is but a

[56] See, for Nicias: VI. 12. 2: *νεώτερος ἔτι ὤν*; and later: "The affair is important and not one that should be left to young people to be decided about and rashly handled. Now, when I see these young people sitting here to answer that same man's call, I am frightened, and call, in return, to more elderly men. . . ." For Alcibiades: 17. i (*ἡ ἐμὴ νεότης*) and 18. 6 (*διάστασις τοῖς νέοις ἐς τοὺς πρεσβυτέρους*) with his proposition of uniting young and elderly people.

[57] This was March, 423.

hint: the servant seems to think that Hippolytus' stern attitude in judging between gods is a sign of imprudent youth: "One must not imitate the young, when such is their way of thinking," he says.[58] In the *Andromache*, the criticism is sharper; it bears on Hermione's demands and cruelty: "Alas," complains Andromache, "youth is a bad thing for mortals and it is bad too when one who is young has what is not rightly his" (184–185).[59] In the *Suppliant Women*, the criticism has turned into political digression, when Theseus suggests that Adrastus has acted wrongly, "led astray by young people" (232); he adds, as something general: "Young people, enjoying honors, develop wars, regardless of justice and with the result of destroying lives in the city: one does it in order to be a general, another in order to be insolent, thanks to the power he owns, and another for profit, not considering the people and what they may suffer from such treatment." This description, which has nothing whatever to do with the action, is obviously inspired by actuality. Every single word in it could apply to Alcibiades, and resembles what Nicias, in Thucydides, says about him.[60] The description would also fit many of Alcibiades' friends, who indeed voted for war, against Nicias' prudent advice. Euripides with his pacific tendency might well have resented their attitude and given voice to his resentment in these two last plays, which are particularly in touch with the things and people of the day.

In that case, the slight surprise that we feel at seeing this condemnation of youth would be due to the intrusion

[58] 117; cf. 1114 ff.

[59] Cf. 238.

[60] Cf., for instance, VI. 12. 2: *ἄρχειν ἄσμενος αἱρεθεὶς . . . τὸ ἑαυτοῦ μόνον σκοπῶν . . . ὅπως θαυμασθῇ μὲν . . . καὶ ὠφεληθῇ τι ἐκ τῆς ἀρχῆς.*

of everyday life and politics in Euripides' trend of thought. Even there, it will be noticed that it comes in without real contradiction. When Euripides has to blame youth, he does it from the point of view of prudence, not of heroic purity. Only he does not always think of prudence, and his poetry does not center on it.

If this is so, we finally meet with two kinds of evolution. One is superficial, linked with everyday events, and it changes according to their pressure.[61] The other is deeper, perhaps more unconscious, and certainly more regular. Yet it would be difficult not to link it also, on another level, with the history of events. This has been suggested in each individual study, as we noticed a sort of parallelism: Aeschylus' theological faith in justice coincided with the city's dramatic recovery from an invasion that violated both piety and justice; Sophocles' moral refusal of change came from a man who formed his ideas when Athens was boldly facing the Greek world and believing in her own achievements; Euripides' interest in man's miseries and his drifting fortunes coincided with the excess of democratic individualism, with the evils of war, with the impending threat against the power of Athens.[62] The general evolution of things prompted the general evolution of thought. And in a city where each citizen was

[61] But there is no contradiction, of course: the excesses of youth only show up from time to time, as the necessary sequel of the new influence of youth.

[62] It should be remembered that most of Sophocles' plays were performed at the same time as Euripides'; but there was a difference in age, of about ten years, in a time of quick changes, when ten years made an important difference. Euripides heard of the Persian wars only by hearsay; and we know, nowadays, that this may mean a great deal.

so passionately attached to the community, it is no wonder that each man's philosophy should reflect the city's common experience.

It is all the more remarkable that each part of this particular experience finally grew into a new progress on the way leading to our modern philosophy and psychology of time. The common experience of Athenian politics turned into inner dialectics and spiritual discoveries, as could only happen with the Greeks. For that very reason, we cannot do without them.

The Messenger Lectures

In its original form this book consisted of six lectures delivered at Cornell University in April 1967, namely, the Messenger Lectures on the Evolution of Civilization. That series was founded and its title prescribed by Hiram J. Messenger, B.Litt., Ph.D., of Hartford, Connecticut, who directed in his will that a portion of his estate be given to Cornell University and used to provide annually "a course or courses of lectures on the evolution of civilization, for the special purpose of raising the moral standard of our political, business, and social life." The lectureship was established in 1923.

Index

I. Passages in Greek Tragedies

[The figures at the left of the columns refer to lines in the plays; those at the right, to pages of this book. Italicized numbers indicate that the passage in the book deals more at length with this section of the play and contains several references to the text of the tragedy. Fragments are referred to, on the whole, according to the numeration in Nauck, which has the practical advantage of giving all our authors together.]

AESCHYLUS

Agamemnon, 12-13, *14-15*, 77-*81*, 109, 146

1 ff.	64
58	61
72-83	146, 162
106-107	46, 147
177	67
180	68
196	64
229	46
251-252	66
462 ff.	62
504	64
551 ff.	95
563	64
700 ff.	62
727	108
763 ff.	62
894	44
928-929	94
976-977	47
983	48
983 ff.	65
1337	70
1388	64
1460	61
1479	66, 70
1484	70
1535	70
1560 ff.	60
1570-1576	70
1619	68, 147-148

Choephoroi, 13, *15*, 26-27, 76-77

22	64
48	61
61 ff.	62
66	61
66-67	27

Aeschylus, *Choephoroi* (cont.)
126 61
204 67
313-314 60
382 ff. 62
464-465 65
470 64
646 66
805 66
886 27
935 64
955 64-65
963 65
965 54, 57
1009 67
1012 71
1024 47
1074-1076 69-70

Eumenides, 13, *15*, 27, *149-150*
38 147
79 ff. 18
238 70
261 61
269 ff. 60
276 68
286 45, 53, 70
378 47
451 70
690 ff. 69
832 70
853 42, 48
918 54
1001 69

Persians, 12, *13*, 26, *73-74*, 79, 137
64 42
171 145
264-265 148
433 92
454 65-66
681-682 145
739-741 16
741 65
744 148
782 148
821-822 66
829-831 148, 150
840 120
852 ff. 146

Prometheus, 13, 69, *74-75*, 79, 95, *148*, 150
10 68
23 ff. 64
94 63
436 ff. 31
705-741 64
741 63-64
746 92
774 16, 63
788-819 64
853 63
955 149
981 45, 53, 60, 68, 70
1020 63

Seven against Thebes, *14*, 63, 71-72, *75-76*
118 54
288 47
622 147
682 70
686 149

Suppliants, *14*, *27*, 108
162 74
177 144
538 74
617 68
681 152
707 144
775 147
1057 65

Fragments
362 46
400 144

Euripides
Alcestis, *21*
381 54, 132
606-740 *165-166*
1036 134
1085 54
1085-1087 132
1159 ff. 119

Andromache, 8, *22-23*, *164*
5 128
84 124

Euripides, *Andromache* (cont.)
184-185 169
238 169
274 ff. 30
645 161-162
774-784 138-139
1009 ff. 30

Bacchae
201 46
282 133
820 124
882 ff. 114
889 57
895-896 117

Electra
504 133
578-579 125
585 126
938 ff. 121
952 126
1157 127
1308 126

Hecuba, 30, 165
61 128
285 118
342-582 166
346 ff. 136
357 128
579-580 136
629 ff. 30
809-810 128
914 ff. 129

Helen, 23
566 126
625, 645 126
1232, 1468 126

Heracles, 22, *164-165*
94 123
107 162
506 ff. 120
506-507 55
510 118
637-700 *159-160*
669 ff. 121
678 147
702 123
777 ff. 114-115
805 51, 117
869 125
941 125
1223 138
1334-1335 138

Heraclidae, 130, *163-164*
38 137
167 162
314 138
433-434 129-130
500-607 135, 166
588 135
624 136
702 ff. 161
898-900 119
900 37

Hippolytus, 167
117 168-169
252 116, 158
369 119
375 44, 125
430 51, 117
525 ff. 30
907 119
1051 51, 117
1102 ff. 119-120
1114 ff. 169
1117-1118 132
1181 125
1322 117

Ion, 23, 167
403 124
575 134
659 134
876 161
1042 161
1130 124
1425 127
1614-1615 115

Iphigeneia in Aulis, 8
419, 636, 640, 660 127
694 133
815 123
1099 124

EURIPIDES, *Iphigeneia in Aulis* (cont.)
1375 ff. 136
1531, 1606 136

Iphigeneia in Tauris, 23
258 127
1117-1122 129

Medea, *8-9*, *10-11*, 21
627 ff. 30
904 ff. 134

Orestes, 23
213 133
234 125
475, 485 127
976 ff. 120
980 119
1201 132

Phoenician Women
64 ff. 133
166, 295, 305 126
367 126-127
528-530 158
543-546 91
834-1018 167
872 ff. 133
1043 127
1545 162-163

Rhesus
559 124
893 116

Suppliant Women, 37, 168
86 133
91 23
165-166 165
195 ff. 31
232-237 169
314, 372, 374 138
419 116, 158
561 138
786-788 54
953 120
1108 160
1118 45, 161
1118-1119 160
1169 ff. 138
1178 138, 139

Trojan Women, 9, 23-24, 30, 165
192 ff. 162
1060 ff. 129
1188 128

Fragments
22 121
23 161
25 162, 163
42 57
52 55
60 51, 117, 118
112 52, 117
222 37, 117
223 115
273 120
282 160
285 129
291 116, 158
303 37, 39, 51, 117, 118
304 120
342 133
344 166
362 115
420 119
441 42, 118
453 160
508 158
509 163
510 158
575 52, 160
585 139
594 38-40
619 116, 158
637 160
733 117
773 55
799 134
800 115
804 161
805 160
807 161
1072 134

FRAGMENTA ADESPOTA
508 45
509 51
510 55, 56, 116

SOPHOCLES
Ajax, *19-20*, *94*
131-132 89, 102
193 111
306 111
399 96
414-415 123
473 152
485-595 7-8
552 ff. 151
554 152
581-582 134
622 46
646 ff. 98-99
647 50
670 ff. 91
711 133
713 53, 95
713 ff. 100-101
748 ff. 18
801 18
1077-1078 104
1266 ff. 101
1359 101-102

Antigone, 29, 104
74-75 105
281 154
332 ff. 31
450 ff. 96, 104
582 ff. 92
593 ff. 88
607 95
609 96
625 88-89
635-765 *156*
681-682 153
726 155
790 96
823 29
856 88
944 ff. 29
987 96
1078 89
1156 ff. 94
1350 ff. 88

Electra
179 55, 101
330 ff. 104
478, 489 19
614 155
616 ff. 155
781 52
985 105, 137
1013 105
1083-1085 105
1337-1338 19
1364 91
1368, 1389, 1397 19
1463 151
1464 105
1505-1506 88

Oedipus at Colonus, 19, *20-21*, 29-30, 103-104, 137, 138
7 44, 95
7-8 151
91 18
103 19
394, 567-568 95
607-609 93, 95, 99-100
609 54, 95
618 37, 52
735 155
751 155
804-805 151, 154
930 42, 154
959, 1116 155
1211 ff. 101
1211-1248 *151-152*, 159
1245 ff. 92
1453 ff. 56, 93
1536-1537 88

Oedipus Rex, 88, *108-110*
73 19
156 91
289 19
865 ff. 96
1050 19
1082 46
1186 ff. 94

SOPHOCLES, *Oedipus Rex* (cont.)
1213 56
1529-1530 94

Philoctetes
15 19
96 ff. 157
199-200 18
235 96
285 42
503 ff. 95
676 ff. 29
878 133
902-903 105
1419-1420 104
1467 54

Trachinian Women, 102, 103
94 ff. *90-93*
114 ff. 89-90
141 ff. 151
161 ff. 16-17
440 101
497 ff. 28
945-946 94
1021 133
1045-1047, 1074-1075 19
1169 48
1169 ff. 17

Fragments
59 45, 108
63 153
194 150
238 133
239 150
280 50-51, 108
375 133
447 153
512 152
588 89
603 150
787 91
808 153
832 51, 108
863 153
864 150
868 100
575 P 91

II. Other Greek Authors

Archilochus, 96, 146
Aristophanes, 35, 40, 57, 168
Aristotle, 6-7, 10, 25
Athenaeus, 59

Bacchylides, 36, 37, 108

Clemens of Alexandria, 40
Critias, 38-41, 133

Democritus, 143

Epimenides, 75

Heraclitus, 4, 36, 96-97
Herodotus, 94, 96, 153-154
Hesiod, 4, 37, 143
Homer, 3, 6-8, 92, 139, 141, 146

Mimnermus, 159

Orphica, 34-39

Pherecydes, 35
Pindar, 4, 6, 36, 37, 42, 44, 47, 48, 50, 51, 52, *53*, 54, 55, 56, 61, 96, 108, 127, 129, 133, 139
Plutarch, 60
Proclus, 34, 38

Simonides, 54, 56, 159
Solon, 36, 61, 107, 143, 148

Thales, 4, 36, 51, 107
Theognis, 36, 107, 152
Thucydides, 82-84, 129, 139-140, 168-169

Xenophon, 108

A.L. OLIVIERA MEMORIAL LIBRARY
3 1782 00164 2384